GPS

THE EASY WAY

BY
DAVID BRAWN

Ask not "What is GPS?"
Ask
"What can GPS do for me?"

GPS - The Easy Way

First published - March 2003
Copyright © 2003

Published by
Discovery Walking Guides Ltd
10 Tennyson Close, Northampton NN5 7HJ,
England

Map sections used in examples
Map sections are from OS Explorer 223 map and
OS Landranger 141 map published by Ordnance
Survey.

Front Cover Illustration
Section of OS Explorer 223 map with GPS Track
and Waypoints added by the author.

Rear Cover Photograph
The author at work (!) researching the new 'Arenas
Negras' walking route in Las Cañadas, Tenerife;
Mount Teide in the background.
Copyright © Ros Brawn 2003.

ISBN 1-899554-46-7

Text and illustrations © David Brawn 2003

Contents

THE AUTHOR

David Brawn is joint CEO of Discovery Walking Guides Ltd and The Indestructible Map Company Ltd. His first walking route 'Geranium Walk' was published in 1988 and this 'urban experience' of Playa las Americas/Los Cristianos in Tenerife has been walked by millions of strollers. David was previously published, Introducing Accounting and Examination Success, before compiling the first 'Warm Island Walking Guide' for Tenerife South in 1993.

Since 'Tenerife South Walking Guide' David & Ros Brawn have authored walking guides for Tenerife North & West, La Gomera, La Palma, El Hierro, Lanzarote, Gran Canaria, Alpujarras, Malta, Gozo, Madeira, Ibiza, Menorca, and Mallorca. Recent walking guide books include Walk! La Gomera, Walk Tenerife South, 34 Tenerife Walks and 34 Menorca Walks.

David is a member of the British Cartographic Society and was instrumental in the map survey, research and design programme that has resulted in Tour & Trail Maps at 1:40,000 scale for walkers; Drive Touring Maps; the amazing Indestructible Maps; and a new series of Walkers' Maps at 1:25,000 scale.

David Brawn enjoys discovering new walking routes, but dislikes 'follow the leader' walking, and he knows a little bit about GPS Navigation.

David Brawn at work researching "34 Tenerife Walks"
GPS in hand.

Foreword

At Discovery Walking Guides (DWG) we have been using GPS navigation systems since well into the last millenium. GPS units have been adorning shop windows and shelves for the last decade. For DWG GPS has proved to be a revelation in accurately describing walking routes and leading to us surveying and designing our own maps, but few others have realised the benefits of using GPS land navigation in the walking world.

Out researching walking routes we have met thousands of walkers but only a handful are carrying a GPS, and of those we have yet to meet one who is getting anywhere near the benefit we get from GPS use. GPS - The Easy Way is an easy to read way for you to get the same benefits that we get from GPS.

Hand held GPS units are in shops and are advertised to walkers, cyclists and a wide range of outdoor adventurers. Shops stock GPS units so they must be selling these units to someone, so why don't we see them being used in the great outdoors?

We suspect that there are '000s, or tens of thousands, of GPS units consigned to hibernating in UK 'sock drawers'; unused and little understood. GPS manuals and books are written for a yachting/US market, adding to the confusion of how to use this technology for land navigation. GPS - The Easy Way, with its Ordnance Survey examples, provides the missing link which can liberate those 'sock drawer hibernaters'.

'Personal Navigator Files' are a revolutionary new product designed specifically for use with GPS units. Walking routes described to a five-metre accuracy every step of the way. DWG's '34 Walks' books combined with 'Tour & Trail', or 'Walkers' Maps', plus 'Personal Navigator Files' (PNFs) combine to produce the most accurate land navigation package ever produced. PNFs are set to revolutionise how walkers navigate both in DWGs European destinations and in the UK's popular walking regions. If you had no other reason to buy GPS - The Easy Way then knowing the technology which underpins PNFs, and how those PNFs are produced, would be reason enough.

"A Compass points North"

but

"A GPS tells you where you are, where you have been, and can show you where you want to go."

1. What is GPS?

A. Satellite Navigation

GPS is the abbreviated version of "Global Positioning System" used to describe devices which use the transmissions of navigation satellites to determine their position on, or above, the earth's surface. The earth is ringed by a system of navigation satellites, each designed to transmit on certain

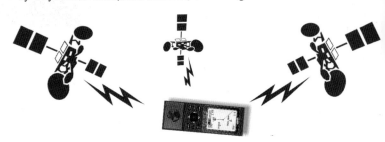

frequencies. By interpreting the transmissions   from 4 or more navigation satellites the GPS receiver can pin-point its position on the ground or in the air, also using the interpretation to calculate the altitude of the receiver.

As with many scientific advances the development of satellite navigation was sponsored by the military to improve their accuracy in delivering munitions; GPS development being closely linked to the development of long distance cruise missiles of exceptional accuracy. Put simply, if you know the co-ordinates of the target a GPS system will guide you to that target with an accuracy of 1-5 metres.

America was the first to commission and launch a series of navigation satellites (NAVSTAR), and as a result commercial applications of satellite navigation have been American led. Russia also has a system of navigation satellites but nobody produces commercial equipment to use their transmissions, while Europe is thinking about launching its own satellite system. Amongst the first commercial applications of satellite navigation and GPS receivers was for ocean navigation. At a stroke the problems of determining your position in a featureless mass of sea were solved. Out went the old methods of sun and star sightings, combined with dead reckoning to give an estimated position, to be replaced by a truly accurate positioning system. In the 1980s GPS swept through commercial sea transport and pleasure sailing, but has had little impact in other non-military activities.

B. Perceptions of GPS

Essential for Yachting,
but not of interest to Walkers!

The MD of a major UK publisher told us over lunch, which he was paying for, that he wouldn't even think of taking his yacht out of the marina unless both his main GPS and hand-held GPS were working correctly. He then went on to tell us that he could not see why GPS would be an important part of guide books for walkers! John was right about sailing but completely wrong about walking, but his thoughts show just why GPS has not taken off big-time for land navigation.

If you are out of sight of land then compass readings, dead reckoning, plus sun and star sights only give you an estimate of your position; and in bad weather you've only got the compass and dead reckoning! Make a mistake in these circumstances and the result can be disaster, so you buy the best navigation system available and as a result 99% of sailors use GPS.

By comparison less than 1% of UK walkers, cyclists and drivers use a GPS system and we think the reason for so little GPS use is that they are never out of sight of land. If they make a mistake in navigation they are unlikely to be dashed onto the rocks. Take a wrong turning and all you have to do is stop, work out your position on a map and then correct your route. Of course not everyone is blessed with good navigational skills and every year we get stories of people who drove out to the shops and ended up in Dorset, but for most of us map based land-navigation has served us well.

C. GPS Accuracy

GPS receivers cycle through the satellite transmissions they are receiving to constantly recalculate the receiver's position. Typically we quote an accuracy of 5 metres for our survey research and regard an accuracy of 10-20 metres to be practical for land navigation. Actual accuracy can be as good as 1 metre in circumstances where you have a modern GPS unit with a clear view of a number of satellites, such as on the high mountain ridges of our Canary Islands research we can have up to ten satellites in view, all with strong signal strength.

GPS manufacturers typically quote accuracies of 15 metres in normal use, 1-5 metres with DGPS corrections, and 100 metres when Selective Availability is switched on. In our experience these quoted resolutions are conservative and will be easily achieved by modern GPS units.

D. Causes of GPS Inaccuracy

a. Selective Availability

This is a system whereby the US military can degrade the satellite transmissions to reduce GPS accuracy for the enemy while the US military corrects for the degradation to give its own forces 5 metre accuracy. During President Clinton's terms in office Selective Availability was switched off giving us all the same precision as the military.

DGPS is a method of overcoming the inaccuracy due to Selective Availability by having a DGPS receiver, linked to your normal GPS unit, which receives a reference transmission from a ground transmitting station to correct for attenuation of the satellite signals. Ground transmitting stations cover many coastal regions to aid shipping navigation but as with the satellites they work on line-of-sight, which is OK over the ocean but a real problem on land when you lose the transmission when the transmitter goes out of sight.

b. Mountain and Building Shadows

GPS relies on line-of-sight transmissions so whenever satellites go out of sight your GPS throws a wobbler and starts moaning, in the form of an insistent peeping, about "poor GPS coverage". This will only happen when you have fewer than four satellites in view, which can happen when you get alongside a mountain, building or even a very large tree. If you do lose the GPS signal then moving away from the object by just a few metres can bring the satellites back into view. In deep canyons, such as Barranco de Masca and Barranco del Infierno in Tenerife, GPS reception can be very poor and the same can apply to narrow streets of tall buildings. Indoors GPS does not work at all!

c. Leaf Cover

Modern myths have grown up around GPS navigation and one of these is the "wet leaves on the trees" explanation of poor GPS reception in forest regions. While nobody has scientifically tested this idea we think the poor reception is due to "trunk blocking" rather than "wet leaves". In La Gomera's wet Laurel forest we usually get good reception under the fairly dense leaf canopy, while Madeira's Eucalyptus trees with large trunks and small leaves cause signal problems. Although the jury is still out we are sticking to "trunk blocking" being the cause of poor GPS reception in forest areas.

d. Body Blocking

One of the most common causes of poor GPS reception comes from putting the GPS in your pocket. The patch aerials in hand-held GPS units need to see the satellites and your own body can act as a block on the signals. Unfortunately hand-held GPS units are normally designed to be used horizontally, on a yacht chart table, and work best when carried in your hand.

Having suffered poor signals by putting the GPS in my shorts/trouser pocket I have now attached the case to a D-ring on the straps of my backpack so the GPS is mounted close to shoulder level; this seems to work better than wearing the case on my belt.

e. Impatience

If you are using your GPS to record where you have been then curb your impatience to be "off and away" at the start of your route. When your GPS is switched on it takes some time to acquire the satellite transmissions. If you move off before your GPS has full satellite acquisition it will make a guess of where it is based upon its last position when it was last switched on. This can be a long way from your actual start point.

Acquisition times can be up to 5 minutes where the GPS has to calculate a completely new position more than 100 kilometres from its last used position, and up to a minute where you are switching on relatively close to where the GPS was last used. Stopping during a route you might want to switch off the GPS to save batteries; satellite acquisition when restarting in the same position can be as quick as 15 seconds.

After switching on most GPS units go to a Navigation screen showing the unit's position, but this does not mean that you have full satellite acquisition. Before moving off do check the Satellite screen to make sure you have acquired four or more satellite transmissions.

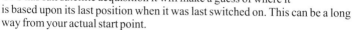

E. GPS versus "Map & Compass" navigation accuracy

GPS accuracy can be as good as 1 metre on the earth's surface and all modern GPS units will meet our (DWG) required field standard of 10-20 metres except when there is poor satellite reception. So how does this compare with navigational accuracy using the traditional "Map & Compass"? The best non-GPS navigational aid, in our opinion, is a set of sighting binoculars with a built in compass; a good quality pair costs more than a GPS unit. Out in the countryside you take bearings on known landmarks, allow for the magnetic deviation, and then plot your sight lines onto a map, and where the lines cross, that is where you are. This is easy as a classroom exercise using assumed bearings but out in the real countryside it is very different.

Using a normal compass is less accurate than a sighting compass, which in turn is less accurate than sighting binoculars. Once you have your bearings where are you going to lay down your map to plot the sight lines? Anyone who has tried plotting their position in windy, or worse, weather will appreciate that the opportunities for error are quite large; and what if you can't see any identifiable landmarks because of the rain/fog/cloud?

5 metres, 10 metres and 20 metres sound large distances when we are talking about accurate systems of navigation. To put these in perspective consider the OS 1:25,000 scale and 1:50.000 scale maps, plus Harvey's 1:40,000 scale maps,

commonly used by outdoor adventurers in the UK. If navigation was only accurate to 100 metres then it would mean that where you think you are on the map is actually 4 millimetres away from where you actually are on a 1:25,000 scale map; on 1:40,000 it is an error of 2.5 millimetres, and at 1:50,000 scale it is an error of 2 millimetres.

 Even at our greatest allowance for GPS inaccuracy of 20 metres this is only 0.8mm, 0.5mm or 0.4mm on 1:25,000, 1:40,000 and 1:50,000 scale maps; less than the size of pen/pencil point most people use to mark their position. When it comes to knowing where you are on the earth's surface only the very best "Map & Compass" navigator would get anywhere near the accuracy of a GPS, and the GPS does this calculation every second while you are moving so whenever you need to know your position it is there instantly.

E. Modern GPS Myths

 People hold strong views on how you should navigate, and these views get even stronger when held by UK walkers. Often these views are not formed on a logical basis but come from untested ideas combined with a lack of knowledge about the alternatives.

On the sea everybody has voted with their wallet and installed GPS to the extent that if you said you were going to cross an ocean using sextant and compass alone you would be regarded as certifiable.

"Map & Compass" navigation is in the same league with Morse Code, which has also disappeared from use at sea since the creation of the satellite phone. As GPS users we are often amazed by the walkers we meet during our research and the views they hold; so here are a few howlers,

"GPS will make you fall in a barranco/canyon." or "off a cliff."

This comment came from a friend and very experienced walker that we were considering asking to write a walking guide book for us. Knowing that we wanted the pin-point accuracy of GPS we were lucky to find an excellent writer and walking researcher who was interested in testing our GPS survey systems. **34 Alpujarras Walks** is the result, a modern classic of a walking guide book that sets new standards of accuracy and interesting descriptions. You will see a lot more of Charles Davis' walking research in the future, all of it GPS accurate, and Charles has never fallen over a cliff.

People confuse the GOTO function of a GPS used for ocean navigation with navigating on land, and assume that the GPS makes you go in straight lines, or perhaps they think that the mighty weight of a GPS (280 grams) will unbalance us near dangerous precipices.

"GPS isn't proper navigation."

This came from another publisher MD friend who has recently published a book on navigation. The book has received good reviews and sells well, we hear; but it does not contain one word about how to use a GPS.

"Map & Compass" navigation is all very boy scouts, Baden Powell, climbing Everest in the 50s, crossing the north African desert, the bomber navigator in a WWII movie, and this image is very difficult to shake off. If you want an accurate navigation system ask those professionals who need precise navigation; they all carry GPS.

"It's just a toy, I know all the walks round here."

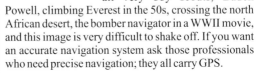

This was said to us by the only member of a walking group with a GPS, when we caught up with them at Lomo de las Lajas, a spectacular mirador viewpoint overlooking southern Tenerife.

We were explaining to some of the group how we (DWG) research our walking routes and saying how accurate GPS is for recording routes. We were directed to the poor soul with the new GPS and when I asked him how he was doing with his GPS, which he had been showing to others in the group, he said **"Oh, I haven't read the manual yet, and any way I know all the walking routes round here."** Realising that he had already put a great walking boot through his reputation he tried to redeem himself, **" Oh, and I was seventy last week."**.

Well age is no defence, and many of the GPS myths, in our opinion, come from people who have bought GPS receivers and then have no idea how to get any useful information out of them - **"but out of ignorance shall come forth knowledge"**.

This gentleman did have one big influence on GPS by inspiring me to find time to compile "GPS The Easy Way" to save people like him from embarassment.

2. Getting Started with your GPS

A. Start Up & Basic Functions

There it is, all shiny and new, the little gizmo that is going to change how you navigate. But what do you do with it?

First tidy up the wrapping paper. A lot of GPS units are given as Christmas, Birthday and Leaving presents (hopefully not as a 'get lost' gesture) so you get the standard package of GPS reciever, case, batteries, manual, guarantee and a few bits of bumpf. As all real men know (most GPS units are bought by men or for men) manuals are for wimps and the first thing you do with any new technical gizmo is to press all the buttons and see what happens. Luckily this is unlikely to cause your GPS any problems but it is not going to help you understand what your receiver can do.

Whether you read the manual, or not, the first things to do with your GPS are;

- check that it has batteries in it, and that they are fitted the right way round, and that the battery compartment is properly closed; a common cause of GPS unreliability many people overlook.

- now go outside. OK, so its Christmas morning and the weather is lousy but there is no point playing with your GPS indoors; this instrument is for 'outdoor navigation' and does not work indoors unless it is connected to your PC which is 'GPS Advanced Use'.
We are sure that many GPS users are put off by trying to play with their gizmo indoors when new and getting very frustrated. Also, going outdoors gets you out of the way.

- when you are away from tall buildings and large trees with a clear view of the sky turn your GPS on, usually the 'bulb' button 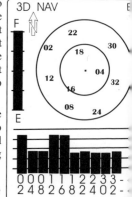 and hold it down until the display lights up. Stay in one place so that your GPS can find where it is on the Earth.
Your GPS was probably made on the other side of the planet and fresh out of its comfy box it is going to feel very disorientated.
After the opening screen, or screens, it should go to the 'Satellite screen' to start acquiring satellite signals. As this is the first time you have switched it on it will need to 'initialise' itself; 'find out where it is' in normal language. A second screen will come above the 'satellite page' asking you to 'choose init method'. Use the arrow buttons to move the bar to 'Autolocate' and press **ENTER** button.
Now put your GPS down where you can see the screen. It can take a good 5 minutes for a GPS to receive enough satellite signals, decode them and work out where it is. This is probably not the exciting 5 minutes you were expecting.

When your GPS has completed its first 'initialise'

your 'Satellite screen' should show a full battery capacity, satellite numbers ranged across the inner and outer circles, and a black bar showing signal strength above each satellite number.

In UK you are likely to have 4-6 satellites with good signal strength while we often have 9 high strength signals when on high ridges in the Canary Islands. Having completed its first 'initialise' your GPS will have much quicker satellite acquisition the next time you switch it on, typically less than a minute. It can be important to remember that until the GPS has acquired four or more satellite signals it is 'technically confused' and can give some strange readings if you are moving before achieving full acquisition.

B. Pressing Buttons & Moving About

Now your GPS is up and running you can scroll through the main GPS screens by pressing the **PAGE** button or **QUIT** button. In Garmin 12 this goes;

Satellite screen - Position screen - Map screen - Navigation screen - System screen - Satellite screen

Having scrolled through the pages select the Map screen. Your current position is shown by the cursor in the lower centre of the screen. Now go for a walk - your local park or streets are a good location - which will involve plenty of changes of direction and recrossing your earlier route. Hold the GPS in your hand trying not to shield it from the satellites and as you walk you will see your track being recorded on the GPS Map screen.

If you bump into something while watching the GPS screen it is a quick reminder that GPS systems were primarily designed for sailors on the open ocean rather than walkers, cyclists and drivers who need to be watching where they are going most of the time!

Each time you change direction, such as at a path or street junction, mark a 'Waypoint' on your GPS pressing **MARK** at the change of direction. A 'Mark Position' screen will come up. Don't worry about any items on this screen at this time, press **ENTER**. Now that Waypoint position is recorded in your GPS memory. Note that the position is recorded when you press **MARK** and is put into the GPS memory when you press **ENTER**.

If you do not wish to record the Waypoint after pressing **MARK**, then press **PAGE** and your GPS will forget the waypoint.

Half an hour of bumping into things, or people bumping into you when you stop abruptly to record a Waypoint, or look at the screen, should be enough.

Your GPS 'Map screen' should show the Track that you have walked with a number of Waypoints which have been recorded in your GPS memory.

Now stand somewhere out of the way and use the arrow keys to move the highlighted bar onto the 'map scale' and press **ENTER**. Expand the screen scale to 1 nautical mile (its that yachting again) and assuming you have walked a compact area you will see the route you have walked as the dark line and the waypoints as numbered symbols. Hopefully the pattern on your GPS Map screen is recognisable as the route you have walked.

Now we come to the real limitation of a GPS receiver on its own. You have recorded a Track and Waypoints but it is stuck in your GPS. Unless you can either download the information or input more information into your GPS there is very little you can do with the Track and Waypoints stored in your GPS' memory.
There is one thing that you can do with the information, and that is turn around and follow your Track back to your start point. The ability to walk/bike/drive back to where you switched on your GPS is an important feature and could even be a lifesaver in severe conditions.

If you have remembered to bring the manual with you then try the GOTO function; on a Garmin simply press the button and your Waypoint List is displayed. Use the arrow buttons to move the highlight bar to a Waypoint and press . Your GPS goes back to the Map screen so press and up will come the Navigation screen in either its Compass or Road form.

Both types of Navigation screen tell you;

- compass bearing to the selected waypoint.
- distance to the waypoint.
- your compass track over the ground (if moving).
- your speed over the ground (if moving).

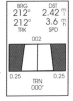

This all looks quite useful until you realise that the course your GPS is telling you to follow is a straight line and takes no account of obstacles in the way! This is OK at sea but on land strictly following the GOTO route can have you bumping into trees, buildings, fences etc. It may also order you to 'fall off a cliff, plunge into a canyon etc'; that is how GPS myths start.
There is only one use I have ever found on land for the GOTO GPS function and that is the very obscure activity of trying to find free-flight model aircraft (don't ask now, see 'Unusual GPS Uses' later).

C. Summary of GPS Basics

Switching On.
- GPS does not work indoors (except in Simulator mode).
- When switched on your GPS needs time to 'initialise', and this acquisition of satellite signals can take up to 5 minutes in a new location.
- Moving your GPS before acquisition, four or more black bars on the satellite page, will confuse the GPS and cause it to record an incorrect position.

Recording Positions.
- Your GPS will record where it is taken and it does this with a high degree of accuracy, unless the Track Recording is turned off.

- You can easily record positions of interest as Waypoints.

Using Recorded Information

- You can follow the Track backwards to the start point where you turned on your GPS.
- Tracks and Waypoints make pretty patterns on your GPS screen and you can view these patterns at a wide range of scales.
- Unless you can import additional information into your GPS, or download the information you have recorded into GPS software, there is little that you can do with the recorded information.
- Beware of using yachting style functions of GPS, such as GOTO or MOB (Man Overboard), unless you understand their limitations when applied to land navigation.

Initial thoughts on GPS

If people just buy, or receive, the basic package of a GPS receiver and have no other advice there is little chance of them using their GPS effectively. It is all too easy to become frustrated by the little gizmo, or become embarassed at owning a GPS. The likely result of this frustration and embarassment is that the GPS is likely to join those tens of thousands of GPS units which 'hibernate in sock drawers' all over the country.

3. Main GPS Screens

Now that we have walked about with the GPS recording a Track and Waypoints, have a look through the other GPS screens. Do this outside or your GPS receiver will start peeping at you and showing 'fail to initialise', 'poor GPS coverage' warnings. In bad weather the owners of soft-top cars and greenhouses can practice with their GPS in some comfort as glass and fabric have little effect on the satellite signals.

Different GPS manufacturers, and different models made by a manufacturer, may have different screens or different amounts of detail on a particular screen, though the general principles underlying screen displays tend to follow those of Garmin and their 12 model. My comments are based on the Garmin 12XL which I normally use when out walking. To move from one screen to another press ⬛PAGE or ⬛QUIT.

Satellite Screen

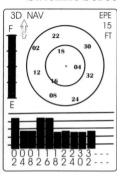

Shows us;
- which satellites the GPS is trying to acquire during initialisation (empty bars)
- when a satellite is acquired the empty bar becomes filled.
- number and signal strength of satellites acquired, along with the satellite number.
- battery power remaining.
These functions are all useful for all GPS users. The functions on the Satellite Screen are preset by the manufacturer and cannot be changed.

Position Screen

Shows us;
- position in Lat/Long or UTM co-ordinates, depending on the setting.
- compass direction (if moving, see also Advanced Features).
- speed.
- track direction from last waypoint.
- time.
then there are optional displays with a choice between,
- Trip, AvSpd, MxSpd, Time, Elapsed.
- Alt, Time, Elpsd, Trip.

The most important information on the Position Screen is **POSITION**; this is what your GPS is all about, the rest are extras.
If you are navigating in the UK then it is best to set your GPS option for Position Format (see Main Menu Screen later) as British Grid and set the GPS Datum to Ord Survey GB. This will mean that the position shown on your GPS can be plotted directly onto an OS map; very useful, and far more accurate than using compass sightings. Personally I prefer Lat/Long positions but this is just a matter of taste.

Compass direction is useful when travelling roughly in straight lines, not so good on zig-zag ascents/descents.
Speed is interesting rather than useful for walkers, more useful for bikers.
Track direction and Time not very useful.
Of the optional displays I have 'Alt', altitude, selected and find it useful when comparing GPS altitude with the altitude shown on a map. Alt is one of the few 'non-Yachting' functions on a GPS!

Map Screen

ZM | 5.0 $\frac{m}{i}$ | PAN | OPT
303°   0.26
176°   2.0

Shows the GPS as a cursor in the lower centre of the screen and the GPS Track being recorded in the Track Log memory, or displaying a track transferred to the GPS memory (GPS Advanced Use). Waypoints stored in the GPS memory are displayed on the Map Screen. At the bottom of the screen are track direction and speed while below the bar are direction to and distance to a Waypoint if you have selected one.

We find this the most useful screen to have up when walking. Seeing where you have been and waypoints appearing after you have pressed **MARK** and **ENTER** is rather satisfying. Speed and direction are interesting rather than useful. Direction and distance to a selected waypoint are for yachting rather than land navigation.

Use the arrow buttons to highlight the sections in the bar.

- 5.0m is the scale of the Map Screen. With this bar section highlighted press the up or down arrow buttons, allowing a few seconds for the screen to re-display; interesting isn't it? On a 12XL the Map Screen scale can range from 0.2 miles to 500 miles as the real size represented by the screen display. As you up the size shown on the Map Screen you should find items pre-loaded by the manufacturer come into view such as major cities. Now press the right arrow button.

- Pan. Pressing the up and down arrows will pan the screen scale in and out. Now press the right arrow button.

-Opt. With this bar section highlighted press **ENTER** for the Options Menu to appear. Select Map Setup and press **ENTER**, the items you want are Map Track Up and Track Log Yes to ensure that your track is being recorded in the track memory and will be displayed on the Map Screen. Press **QUIT** or **PAGE** to go back to the Options Menu.

Select Track Setup and press **ENTER**.

Track Setup is a key screen for us as it shows us how much track memory has been used recording the track so far.
12XL has a track memory of 1024 positions, which doesn't sound much but

we have never got near this amount of memory even on the longest of our walking days. We select the Record option of Wrap which means after recording the 1024 track point it will then replace stored track points by the new points being recorded in number order from number 1. The chances of you ever achieving this Overwrite in a days walking are very remote.

For Method we select Auto which means a track point will be recorded each time we make a change of direction, or if no change of direction has taken place at a fixed time interval.

Clear Log? is the other key function for us in the options menu. Selecting Clear Log? and pressing **ENTER** we are asked if we really want to clear the memory, the default is set to NO to avoid you accidentally deleting your track. After we have downloaded the Track to a PC, and saved it to hard disc and floppy disc, is when we go into the Clear Log? option to clear the GPS Track Log memory.

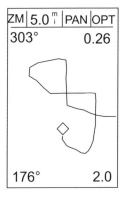

Importance of the Map Screen

Every time we go walking we take a GPS with us, usually a Garmin 12XL or a Garmin 48 (a lovely compact GPS with removable aerial, now unfortunately obsolete), and most of the time we are researching new walking routes, or rewalking our earlier routes.

In the sort of mountainous terrain, and amongst the trees and heather, that feature in DWG walking guides you can be just a few metres from an earlier position without realising how close you are to creating a link; eg from one side of a low ridge to the other. Map Screen displays our earlier Track and recorded Waypoints, so warning us that we are approaching where we walked earlier; for this feature alone I would buy a GPS. Add in a download lead plus GPS software so that I can download the Track and Waypoints into a PC to create the most accurate walking maps available (GPS Advanced Use) and you might begin to see why we regard GPS as an ESSENTIAL tool for walking researchers, and as the most useful tool available for leisure walkers.

As you move the Map screen automatically re-orients itself so that your direction is always towards the top of the screen. Turn a corner, or reverse direction, and you will see the Map screen re-orientate itself to match your new direction.

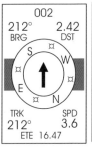
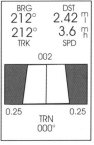

Compass/Road Screen, sometimes called Navigation Page

This screen might have an option of showing a Road in place of a Compass but it is really for yachting. Used in conjunction with the GOTO a 'selected waypoint' the Compass/Road Screen will direct you straight to the waypoint IRRESPECTIVE of whatever is in the way! They call it a Navigation Page but perhaps it should be renamed "Potential Disaster Ahead" page.

GOTO function is useful for hot air balloon support crews to plot the wind direction the balloon is following, similarly for retrieving free flight model aircraft, but it is much safer to use this function on land with the Map Screen rather than the Compass/Road Screen.

Main Menu Screen

MAIN MENU
WAYPOINT
WAYPOINT LIST
NEAREST WPTS
PROXIMITY WPTS
ROUTES
DIST AND SUN
MESSAGES
SETUP MENU
FIND CITY

This is where you can configure most of the GPS functions to suit your own style of GPS use. It is also the screen most likely to be presented differently by different manufacturers, and between different models, depending how you are supposed to access and change the optional settings. Sorry, but this is one aspect where you do need to read the manual for your own GPS.

Running down the 'Main Menu', use the 'arrow buttons rocker' switch, to highlight each bar and then press **ENTER** to access the function menu.

- **WAYPOINT** displays the properties of the selected waypoint. If no waypoint is selected the fields are blank. You can use this Waypoint display to input details manually; just the task for a wet weekend when you can think of absolutely nothing else to do, see 'GPS Advanced Use' for the easy way to input lists of Waypoints. Most GPS give you the opportunity to give each Waypoint a name and a display symbol, though why you should want to do this is unclear to me.

- **WAYPOINT LIST** displays the Waypoints stored in the GPS memory in number order and you can select a waypoint using the 'arrows rocker' key. If you then go to 'Waypoint' you can see, and modify, that Waypoint information. Most important is the 'Delete Waypoints?' bar at the bottom of the screen, selecting this and pressing **ENTER** you will be asked 'what type of waypoints' you wish to 'delete', select an option and press **ENTER**, then you are asked again and warned that the action will 'delete all waypoints'; click the option from its NO default to YES and press **ENTER** and all your Waypoints are deleted from memory!!! This sounds like a major error but this is how you clear the Waypoint Memory once you have stored the Waypoint information in more accessible form, again see 'GPS Advanced Use'.

- **NEAREST WPTS** lists the stored Waypoints in order of distance from your present position. Remember this is in order of straight line distance irrespective of what might be in the way.

- **PROXIMITY WPTS** lists any Waypoints you have designated as Proximity Waypoints in order of straight line distance from your present position.

- **ROUTES** allows you to allocate Waypoints to a numbered Route. You can add a name to the Comment field to help you identify what the Route refers to. Waypoints are posted into the Route and you can then 'activate the route'. Route navigation is very useful for sailing where the Waypoints represent turning points defining legs to be sailed and the Route function can tell you 'estimated time of arrival' based on your speed and shows you the desired track to get to the next waypoint. For walking Routes is still useful, allowing you to store up to 20 Routes of up to 30 Waypoints each (Garmin 12XL spec), in your GPS. Remember these are Waypoints not Tracks and the usual warnings apply concerning straight line navigation on land.

- **DIST AND SUN** shows you the direction and distance between two selected Waypoints, yacht navigation again, plus the time of sunrise and sunset.
  At first I wondered why 'Sunrise and Sunset' get such a prominent display in a GPS until I realised that sightings at these times are important for traditional ocean navigation, though why you want this information in a GPS that tells you exactly where you are on the ocean is another one of the mysteries of GPS design.

- **MESSAGES** is used to remind you of what alarms are set, eg Proximity Waypoints.

- **FIND CITY** is a strange function for someone trying to navigate in the countryside and if I want to know where Denver is I will look it up in an atlas; an example of GPS trying to be all things to all people.

- **SETUP MENU** this is very important. In the Setup Menu you can configure the GPS screens to best suit the type of use you will make of your GPS.

MODE; choose between Normal, PowerSave or Simulator. We select Normal but if you are worried about battery consumption you could select PowerSave. Selecting 'Simulator' will allow you to use the GPS indoors without it worrying about lack of satellite signals, useful when inputting Waypoints but do remember to reset the Mode to Normal or PowerSave afterwards. Now you can work indoors with your GPS if you want to.

NAVIGATION; choose the Position Format you prefer, I like Lat/Long but in UK use Brit Grid. Set the Datum to the one used by the maps where you will be navigating, in UK this would normally be OrdSurvy GB. Choose the units of Distance Measurement, Statute (miles), Nautical or Metric. For UK use of your GPS you will probably find that Position Format 'British Grid', Datum 'OrdSrvy GB' and Distance Measurement 'Statute' as being the most usable Navigation settings.

- **ALARMS SETUP** screen is used if you want your GPS to peep at you when approaching a Waypoint. If you operate in the Map Screen then Alarms seems a bit 'belt and braces'.

- **INTERFACE** is a most important area if you want to graduate to 'GPS Advanced Use' and use your GPS with GPS software or to communicate with any other device; see 'GPS Advanced Use'.

- **LANGUAGE**, select English unless you want to use your GPS as a basic language tutor.

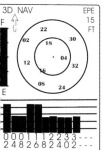

Summary of GPS Screen Displays

Familiarising yourself with the Main Screens and the options you have to configure your GPS to your own style of use is very important, along with realising the limitations of the screen displays and information being presented to you by your GPS. As a walker (main use), biker, driver and retriever of wayward free-flight model aircraft I find GPS a great advantage over other forms of navigation most of the time, but I still feel that current GPS units are a 'dog of bits' in trying to graft on functions to what was originally a navigation system for yachting.

Before you go out and show your GPS to people who haven't got one, make sure you can use the 'page', 'enter', and 'arrows/rocker' switch to confidently navigate through the screens to display the information you want. Do make sure that the System Setup has been set for your own circumstances, and do make sure you have set the GPS to Normal or PowerSave mode before using it outdoors. Showing off your new GPS gizmo to technophobe compassophiles can be an unnerving experience which might make you become a closet GPS user.

Typical of the sort of comments you might get from the technophobe compassophiles are;

At start of a walking route.

"I'm just waiting until I've got all the satellites up."
"You don't have to wait around with a compass."

Showing off Route Navigation or GOTO function

" That'll have you falling over that cliff."

Low batteries, changing batteries.

"you don't need, run out of, batteries with a compass mate."

Find City function.
"I don't need three hundred quids' worth of kit to tell me where London is."

General usefulness.

"What do you mean it doesn't make tea, at that price I'd expect it to make champagne."

4 Let's get Busy, Practical Exercise in GPS use

By now you should be reasonably familiar with your GPS unit. You have taken it for a walk, recording the Track you walked, recording Waypoints and have seen the dangerous limitations of the GOTO function when applied to land navigation. You are now familiar with the GPS Main Screens and the Menus accessed off those screens, along with the important aspects for configuring your GPS.

So now lets get down to some practical use for your GPS.

Practical Aspects of Land Navigation

Most peoples' navigation is by way of a map or atlas. A few people will also use a compass in association with a map for their navigation, but these are far fewer than 'map & compass' navigators would have us believe.

For walking many walkers simply follow the walker in front, with the one at the front being the 'walk leader' who knows the route; this is Ramblers' style walking which is also used by most companies offering walking holidays. Independent walkers usually navigate a route with the help of a guide book possibly containing maps or perhaps using a seperate map; some of them might carry a compass as well, but again relatively few.

As creators of walking guide books (DWG) we try to provide all the navigation information needed for a route within an interestingly written route description. Judging by our fan mail we are very good at this.

We make sure that we give clear directions at each key point (**Waypoint**) of a route including general compass direction, eg **NNE**, along with 'we turn left'. Also we give frequent timings from **0m** at the start to points along the route enabling the guide book user to check their walking speed against ours. This attention to detail has gained us a reputation for 'accurately and interestingly described walking routes'.

We have gone from '**accurate**' to '**extremely accurate**' route descriptions thanks to GPS but you don't need GPS to use our guide books.

The key to successful land navigation is getting to the end of your route having passed through all the points along the way that you wanted to pass through.

If you are a common Rambler (guided walking holiday user) all the navigation skills you need are to get to the start point, and then follow the leader; you will not need a map, compass, guide book or GPS, though all of these can add to your walking experience.

Independent walkers and walking researchers will definitely benefit from using GPS for land navigation. GPS can show you the route back to the start in an emergency, but more importantly it accurately records where you have been and can be programmed for where you want to go.

Discovery Walking Guides '34 Walks' guide books now include GPS Waypoints for all routes with good satellite signal reception, allowing you to manually input those Waypoints into your GPS as a series of Routes before you set out.

Making up a Walking Route

Your GPS is an accurate recorder of where you have been but it would be of much more practical use if you could program it for routes that you propose to travel.

Important Note. In this practical exercise I have chosen North Luffenham airfield, notable for the country's flattest golf course and model aircraft flying, but there is NO PUBLIC ACCESS to the area shown on this map section.

To "Plan a Route" and "Input that Route into your GPS" here is what you do;

- Buy a 1:25,000 scale OS Explorer, or 1:50,000 scale OS Landranger map of the area where you live, or of where you would like to go.

- Familiarise yourself with the "How to give grid reference (British National Grid)" section of the map legend, not forgetting those SK letters identifying the 100,000 metre square .

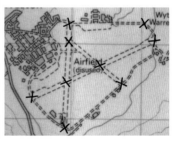

- Decide on a route, preferably returning to your start point, that you would like to walk and mark it on the map, in pencil if you are worried about spoiling the map.

My ' test' route is a figure of eight around North Luffenham airfield and I am using OS Landranger 141 1:50,000 scale map.

- For the route you have chosen calculate a series of Grid References for all the key points along the route. These should be all junctions where you will have a choice of direction, plus main changes of direction and as many other points along the route as you feel you will need to navigate confidently. Number these Grid References in the order that you expect to pass through them.

For North Luffenham airfield I plan to start at the entrance onto the airfield, follow the perimeter track past where it swings right, on to the junction with the main runway, follow the main runway to cross another runway, straight on across another runway, and at the end of the runway I will come onto the perimeter track again. Then I will follow the peri track SE passing another runway on my left to continue on the peri track to the next runway on my left,

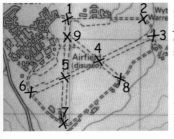

which I take to cross my outward route at the junction of the runways, on to the next junction of runways, and then head north back to my start point.

For this route I have nine key navigation points which I have marked on my map.
Now it is down to calculating the Grid References.

I've identified the 100,000 metre square as SK and each key navigation point's grid reference is:

1 Entrance onto perimeter track	SK 49395 30535
2 Perimeter track swings right	SK 49510 30530
3. Runway junction	SK 49520 30510
4. Runways crossroads	SK 49440 30470
5. Runways crossroads	SK 49390 30450
6. Runway/Peri track junction	SK 49345 30430
7. Runway/Peri track junction	SK 49390 30385
8. Runway/Peri track junction	SK 49470 30445

Note that although my route is expected to pass through 4 again we do not create a new grid reference or Waypoint.

9.Runways junction	SK 49395 30500

Note that in calculating the grid references I find it impossible to plot more accurately than 0.5mm, equivalent to 25 metres at 1:50,000 scale. On an airfield like North Luffenham the perimeter track is normal road width and the runways almost as wide as a motorway, so 25 metre plotting accuracy should not be a problem. Grid

references are calculated to five figures as this is the format for my GPS in Position Format British Grid and Datum Ord Survey GB.

My list of Grid References, calculated from the OS map, have now defined the route I wish to travel so let's put this into the GPS.

- Power up 🔲 your GPS, **PAGE** **PAGE** **PAGE** **PAGE** to **Main Menu** screen, down to select **Set-up Menu**, select **Mode** and select **Simulator** and press **ENTER**. I am assuming you are doing this exercise indoors, it may take some time. Now go to **Waypoint List** and clear any Waypoints stored in your GPS.

Then to **Map Screen**, arrow across to **OPT** **ENTER**, down to select **Track Setup** **ENTER** and down to **Clear Log?** **ENTER** and clear the **Track Log** memory.

- **PAGE** **PAGE** **PAGE** to **Setup Menu Screen,** down to **Navigation** **ENTER**. Now check that you have **Position Format British Grid**, and **Datum Ord Survey GB**.

MAIN MENU
WAYPOINT
WAYPOINT LIST
NEAREST WPTS
PROXIMITY WPTS
ROUTES
DIST AND SUN
MESSAGES
SETUP MENU
FIND CITY

- **PAGE** **PAGE** to the **Main Menu Screen** go to **Waypoint** **ENTER**.

Now we start inputting our **Grid References** as **Waypoints** making sure they are in the same number order. First select the Waypoint Number and using the arrows buttons select number 1. Then arrow down to the OS Grid Reference first letter of the 100,000 metre grid square, **ENTER** and then lots of arrows before we get to the correct first letter, arrow to the next letter and then more arrows to get to the correct second letter. Arrow across to the first number, I did warn you that this could take some time. After interminable 'arrowing 'I have got my first Waypoint on the screen as

1 **.**

SK 49395

BNG 30535

Finally arrow down to **DONE?** and **ENTER**. That is just the first Waypoint, there are still eight more to input for my simple route around North Luffenham airfield.

Once you have manually inputted a long list of Grid References you will easily appreciate the benefits of a PC download lead and GPS software for "**GPS Advanced Use**"!

- When you have finished inputting the Waypoints go back to the **Setup Menu Screen** and reset Mode to Normal or PowerSave and power down **■**.

Your Baptism of Fire; GPS Style

Now we are on the brink of seeing if you have become GPS Accomplished. If you get through this test of your GPS usage you can hold your GPS high and be proud of it.

"But what if I fail the test?"

Well, this is like those tests of Faith where you have to fall backwards into the arms of a friend. Will they be there? Will they be strong enough to catch me?

At some stage you have got to test your accuracy at compiling the information you have programmed into your GPS. You test your accuracy by going out into the great outdoors and using that information to navigate your planned route and get you back to your start point; oops, I didn't say a circular route did I. OK don't panic, if you have planned a linear route that's OK, we'll just follow the route in reverse to get back to your start point.

This is the big one. This is 'Graduation' in GPS

If you can navigate out and back using the Waypoints in your GPS you have mastered the concepts of '**GPS and Map Navigation**'. Never again will you be nervous of confessing to owning a GPS or of taking it out in public. Pass this and you can laugh at those Technophobe Compassophiles, rather than be embarrassed by them.

OK so let's do it.

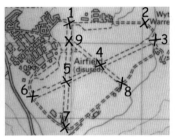

- Go out to the start of your planned route taking the OS map and list of Grid References with you.

- Power up your GPS  and while it is acquiring satellites familiarise yourself with your planned route on the OS map.

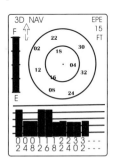

- Sats Up? Check **Satellite Screen**.

- Now for a last minute check before you move off look at your Waypoints against the list of Grid References.

`PAGE` `PAGE` `PAGE` `PAGE` to Main Menu, 'arrow down rocker' to Waypoint, press `ENTER` and check each Grid Reference is correctly recorded as a Waypoint; correct any inputting errors.

- Put away the Grid Reference list, fold up the OS map, and get ready to depart!

- `PAGE` `PAGE` `PAGE` to the Map Screen and adjust the Screen Scale so that you can see Waypoint 002, and hopefully two or three others on the little GPS screen.

- You should be standing at Waypoint 001. Take a deep breath, calm down your nervous heartbeat, and walk towards Waypoint 002.

IF, If, If, If only I'd . . . . .

If you've calculated the Grid References reasonably accurately.
If you've input those Grid References correctly as Waypoints into your GPS.
If you can tear your eyes away from the GPS screen to see where you are walking.

Then you should find your route taking you along as planned, moving from one waypoint to another with the aid of your GPS, feet and eyes. Keep going until you get back to your start point; or for linear routes walk out to the last Waypoint and then turn round and follow your outward track back to the start.

That's right, "Accurate Navigation" without a compass, without reference to a map.

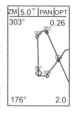

If you did not get back to your start point or had problems navigating using the GPS Map screen see below, '**Reasons for Poor GPS Navigation**'.

Congratulations you have graduated from the 'sockdraw' to become 'GPS Accomplished'.

Not only can you record a GPS Track and Waypoints to describe where you have been; you can plan a route from an OS map, input the information into your GPS, and then use your GPS to navigate the route you had planned. Believe me that is very **GPS Accomplished** by anyone's standards. Now, before we rush down the pub to celebrate, if you could just spend a bit more time we could even complete your post-graduate diploma in GPS navigation so skip down to '**Post-Graduate GPS Navigation**'.

My 'North Luffenham' Exercise

At the airfield I park near the golf clubhouse and walk back to my starting point, which should be Waypoint 1; this is alongside a fairway and parking here could result in dings from wayward golf balls. Heading off eastwards I stroll past the club house and out towards Waypoint 2. An advantage of using an airfield is that my route is very wide compared to a walking trail. I know I can only plot my Waypoints to an accuracy of 0.5mm on the map (1:50,000) equivalent to 25 metres in reality; this would be an accuracy of 12.5 metres if I used a 1:25,000 scale map. With this level of accuracy a wide route helps smooth out my own plotting inaccuracy.

Airfields are almost flat so it is an easy stroll to Waypoint 2, which is approximately where the perimeter track curves right. Round to Waypoint 3 and then I head along the main runway, there is no flying at this old aerodrome, through Waypoints 4 & 5 to reach the perimeter track again at Wayppoint 6. South-east along the peri track curving left at Waypoint 7 past the runway on my left. At Waypoint 8 I turn left to follow the runway, passing through Waypoint 4 a second time before coming to the runway junction at Waypoint 9. Going right a short stroll brings me back to my start point at Waypoint 1 and my Map Screen looks like-

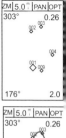

For me it was an easy exercise, except for inputting the Waypoints, as I am navigating in easy conditions and recognise the limitations of my plotting inaccuracies.

Reasons for Poor GPS Navigation

There are a number of possible reasons why your first try at GPS navigation could be less than successful. Run through this list of possibilities to see if they apply;
- Have you calculated the grid references correctly?
- If your Grid References are correct have you input them correctly as waypoints?
- Is your GPS set toDatum Ord Survey GB and Position Format British Grid?
- Was your GPS set toDatum Ord Survy GB and Position Format British Grid when inputting your Waypoints?
- Did you calculate enough Grid References/Waypoints to cover all the navigation decision points in your planned route?
- Did you rely too much on the GPS and not enough on your eyes for obstacles to avoid?

Whatever form of navigation you choose it is only as good as the information that you put into it. This applies as much to GPS as to map, guidebook, map & compass methods of navigating from one point to another.

Post-Graduate GPS Navigation

Congratulations on having planned a route, calculated the Grid References and input them into your GPS as a list of Waypoints, and then having navigated around your planned route using your GPS, feet and eyes. As well as becoming 'GPS Accomplished' you have also recorded your exact route, as the Track Log, while testing your GPS navigation against your planned route.

For your Post-Graduate Diploma I want you to re-walk your route following the track displayed on the Map screen, but with a few deliberate errors.

First though, to stop your GPS overwriting the track you have created, you should turn off the **Track Recording**. **Map Screen**, 'arrow' right to **OPT** press **ENTER**, 'arrow' to **TRACK SET-UP** on the pop-up screen press **ENTER**, 'arrow' down to highlight **WRAP** press **ENTER**, 'arrow' down twice to select **OFF** press **ENTER**, then **PAGE** to bring back the Map screen and check that you are on the largest size of screen; 0.3km on my 12XL.

Now I want you to re-walk your route noting that the screen cursor follows your track from the first time. You should find it relatively easy, or very easy, to follow the track which represents exactly where you walked before. If somebody else had created this Track Log you would now be walking in the same footsteps as they did when the track was created.

Read that last sentence again and something should go PING in your mind!

That's right, if you could use a Track Log of a route in your own GPS you can easily follow the exact route using the Map screen even though you have never been on the route before; and that is just what "**Personal Navigator Files**" are, **Track Logs** and **Waypoints** for walking routes, see later chapter for more details.

OK so following the **Track** on the **Map Screen** is easy, so what happens if you go wrong?

Take a wrong turning, or walk away from your original route, and see what happens on the **Map Screen**.
How far did you have to go from the original track before it was visible on the Map screen that you were going the wrong way?

On our hand-held GPS units we can normally see this error within 5-10 metres of going wrong. This is despite the tiny screens used on hand-held GPS units and the technical specification of a 15 metres RMS accuracy. Basically that little GPS in your hand is the most accurate navigation device available today; tomorrow who knows.

Summary of 'Being GPS Accomplished'

Graduating from our "Baptism of Fire; GPS Style" means that you can confidently;

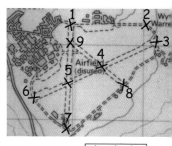

- Plan a UK route that you want to travel using a 'GPS Compatible' map (OS) from which you know the Datum of the map and can calculate the Grid References of the key points you expect to pass through on your route.

- Input those Grid References into your GPS, with your GPS Datum set to the same Datum as the map, as Waypoints.

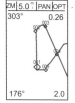

- Use the Waypoint List you have created to navigate from Waypoint to Waypoint using your GPS Map screen and your eyes. Note the eyes, this is real navigation rather than the 'blind' GOTO navigation favoured by GPS manufacturers.

- With an accurately described Track Log stored in your GPS you can exactly follow the Track using your GPS Map screen, and know very quickly whenever you are deviating from the Track. (see **Personal Navigator Files**)

5 Things they don't tell you about GPS

Now that we are 'GPS Accomplished', and I have been largely praising the use of GPS, is perhaps a good time to look at some of the 'downsides' of GPS usage. Some are my own personal beef as a walker using GPS, while others have been gleaned from the **uk.rec.walking** and **sci.geo.satellite-nav** internet newsgroups where they frequently form the basis of discussions.

70s/80s Technology

GPS was originally developed to improve the accuracy of munitions delivery, viz cruise missiles. Unfortunately much of the 70s/80s is still seen in current GPS units with relatively high battery consumption for what they do and very slow (serial port) speeds when communicating with other equipment, see '**GPS Advanced Use**'.

Yacht/Pilot Based GPS

GPS' first commercial uses were developed for ocean and airborne navigation where it replaced sightings, dead-reckoning and compass direction navigation. Current GPS units reflect this design heritage in that manufacturers still bias their manuals towards sailors. Just look at the emphasis on 'Route Navigation' 'MOB Man Overboard' and 'GOTO' functions in your GPS manual. On land you need far more waypoints than the manuals suggest if you are going to navigate sufficiently to graduate as 'GPS Accomplished'.

On the manuals for two of our GPS systems the covers seem to deliberately confuse the unwary. On a marine unit marketed for small power boat use the manual cover shows the Road Screen of the Navigation page, perhaps not so unlikely as it shows the unit heading towards 'cove'. For a hand-held unit marketed for walkers (amongst others) the manual's cover shows the Map Screen at 5.0 miles size and the track as two straight lines equivalent to more than a mile long. As 'Trail Head', 'Bridge' and 'Lake' (how twee) waypoints are shown this presumably demonstrates land navigation. Has anyone navigated one mile on land in a straight line?

Intermittent GPS Operation

Quite a lot of GPS users suffer from their GPS seeming to shut off for no reason, leading to a broken track record and a blank screen just when you want some information from your GPS; at least that is when you notice the phenomena.

Shutting Off when using car electric power.

This used to happen quite often to us when operating 12V GPS units off the cigarette lighter socket in our diesel Land Rover. We finally identified the problem as my driving; there I've said it and I am still a man. Because the diesel motor has so much torque I tend to bumble along dirt roads with the motor at quite low rpm. When we came to, or hit (!), an obstacle I am in too high a gear and the engine almost stalls, resulting in no 12V to the socket and the GPS shutting down. Now we are much more reliable at off-road research as I drive in a lower gear, keeping the engine revs in the 1,500 - 2,500 rpm range, and goodbye to intermittent GPS.

Shutting Off in battery powered hand held GPS units.

Batteries and the battery mountings appear to be the cause of this rather common complaint from people who use their GPS on bikes over rough ground, but it can also happen to walkers.

First thing to check is that you have the battery compartment properly closed. This is particularly important where the door of the compartment is part of the battery circuit.

Second, is there any sideways movement possible for the batteries? Technically it does not matter which AA batteries you use, but in practice there are small size differences between brands. If you suspect that your batteries are 'rattling' about try putting a layer of 'Magic Tape', or similar around each battery to reduce the room for movement.

Third, are the springs holding the batteries strong enough to prevent the batteries losing contact with each other when subjected to vibration or sudden shock? As a crude measure you can try stretching the springs so that the batteries are under greater pressure, but don't go too far or you find you have problems inserting new batteries or in removing old ones.

Elevating GPS

With your GPS turned on and with the Position Screen selected, with the Alt option on, place the unit on a fixed surface and watch the display. Usually your GPS will show changes in altitude and saying it is getting higher even though you know it is not moving. Internet newsgroups ponder this GPS phenomena from time to time with people suggesting various reasons.

Now **PAGE**, **PAGE**, **PAGE**, **PAGE** to the Satellite Screen and look at which satellites you are receiving.

'Elevating GPS' phenomena tend to occur when your GPS has a good view of the sky and is receiving signals from satellites near the horizon; now think triangulation. As your GPS cycles through the satellite signals carrying out triangulations to calculate its position it will get its most accurate fix from the most distant satellites, those near the horizon. Those distant satellites give the best position fix but the worst altitude fix, hence changes in altitude. Why the altitude keeps rising is still subject to debate.

Good Sats, Poor Accuracy.

GPS manuals tell us that we need four or more satellites to operate in 3D mode for an accurate location fix. The assumption is that with four satellites being received you will get an accurate position fix.

Our own experience in the exceptional surroundings of the Barranco de Masca on Tenerife would suggest otherwise. Normally our GPS use is under wide skies with seven to ten satellites showing on the Satellite Screen, giving us exceptional accuracy of position. Barranco de Masca is a very steep canyon surrounded by vertical cliffs and we know that we will soon hit 'poor GPS coverage' when we are deep down in the canyon. Starting from the car park with four satellites up, getting up to five satellites up on a rock outcrop above the bridge and then dropping to four and then three before we get 'poor GPS coverage' going steeply down to the watercourse. GPSing the route back up the head of the canyon I noticed lots of discrepancies compared to our outward track, the path is only 30cms wide in places with no alternative place to walk. So apparently good satellite reception but poor positional accuracy.

The problem is the opposite of 'Elevating GPS'. Surrounded by cliffs we were only using the satellites above 45 degrees, inner ring on the Satellite Screen, which give the worst positional accuracy.

Eyes and Intelligence

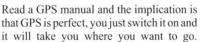

Read a GPS manual and the implication is that GPS is perfect, you just switch it on and it will take you where you want to go. Seldom, if ever, does a manual say anything about you needing to interpret the GPS information against what you are seeing; probably because in yachting you are often surrounded by a lot of nothing. From a GPS manual you would think that navigation was simply a series of straight 'legs' connected by compass directions and nothing gets in the way; quite different to the physical reality you encountered on your "Baptism by Fire" exercise to become GPS Accomplished.

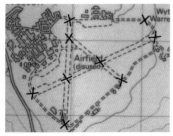

In the real world of land navigation we are constantly reassessing our position and making navigational corrections to avoid hazards which crop up; avoiding bumping into other walkers, going round trees/lampposts rather than bumping into them. Operating in the real world means that we navigate by a combination of pre-planned information; maps and/or GPS routes, which is updated in real-time by your own observations such as 'I will walk around that tree rather than bump into it'. If only GPS manufacturers would include some of the practical aspects of land navigation in their manuals there would not be such a large void between what the equipment promises and what it actually delivers to the average buyer.

Gizmos Eat Batteries

A standard moan in internet newsgroups is about how quickly GPS units use up batteries. This argument, rather than problem, can be exaggerated by which batteries you use. Recently I have given up using what I considered a middle range brand, 60 pence for 4AAs in St James, Northampton, after I found they were only giving 4-5 hours of GPS operation; Ros has bought me a better brand that costs a bit more and it looks like we are back to 24 hours continuous use on a set of 4AAs.

We all get suckered into an expensive bargain at some time. Mine was in buying batteries from a 'Del Boy' stall on Northampton market; 24AAs for a pound is cheap, cheep, cheep! The first 4AAs from this purchase lasted all of 28 minutes!

GPS units are not renowned for their power efficiency, plus battery consumption increases for every extra function that they are performing. Add in an electronic compass and it might look useful but it uses up battery power. Add in a barometric altimeter; again, that looks useful but up goes your battery consumption. Generally every extra function added to the basic GPS engine has to be paid for in power consumption.

This isn't a problem for walkers doing day walks as you put in a new set of batteries when you need them, or recharge those rechargeables overnight, but for hikers who are going to spend days away from civilisation the extra weight of a mass of AAs can be quite a problem. If you are worried about battery consumption, either from expense or weight of spare batteries, then switch off all optional functions, consider using the PowerSave Mode, or settle for a simple GPS unit.

Mountain/Building/Tree, Body Shadowing

GPS manuals point out that you need a clear view of the sky and 4+ satellites to operate in 3D mode for an accurate position fix; true as far as it goes. If you try using your GPS to navigate around the narrow streets and alleys you find in historic towns you will soon find the unit peeping at you and displaying 'poor GPS coverage'. The same goes for deep canyons such as Barranco de Masca and Barranco del Infierno on Tenerife.

Mountains and buildings block out satellite signals but this is hardly mentioned in the manuals, reflecting their yachting background where such obstructions do not exist. Less well known is the shadowing caused by tree trunks unless you do much navigating through forests.

Little talked about is body shadowing caused by where you put your GPS. When I first started using a hand-held GPS I used to either carry it in my hand, inconvenient and impossible when scrambling, or put it in the pocket of my shorts where it often started peeping rather embarassingly due to 'poor GPS coverage'. Using the GPS case clipped on my belt was better but I could still end up with my body shadowing the GPS so much as to get the peeping back.

My own solution to this is to attach the GPS case to a D-ring high on the shoulder strap of my backpack so the unit sits at shoulder level with a clear view of the sky. For most shadowing problems with satellite reception I'm afraid that we just have to live with the limitations of GPS coverage.

Why Do All The Bits Cost So Much?

You can buy a modern GPS unit for around a hundred pounds. Prices then range up through the hundreds for consumer models and then into the thousands for professional equipment. If a fully working modern GPS only costs a hundred pounds where is the justification for charging thirty pounds for a bit of wire that connects the GPS to a computer and external power supply, or twenty pounds for a clip your GPS sits in on the handle bars, and have you seen the price of an external aerial. It seems that once we have a basic GPS, we are paying tens of pounds for items that cost pence to produce, so that we can use our GPS efficiently. Unfortunately accessories are expensive, though they are becoming a bit cheaper as non-GPS manufacturers start producing accessories for the 'after main purchase' market.

Incompatibility between Manufacturers

With computers you have a basic choice between a PC or a Mac. Once you have decided which type you want you are unlikely to change in the future partly because of the expense of the new equipment, but mostly because of the time involved learning new systems and interfaces.

GPS is much the same with manufacturers guarding their patents and only producing products that work on their equipment. Try moving from a Magellan to a Garmin, on to an Eagle, and then on to a Lowrance; or a Trimble if you can afford professional prices.

This incompatibility between manufacturers is breaking down, not by the manufacturers working towards common standards but by independent GPS software developers producing programmes which will accept input from the widely differing ranges of manufacturers standards. With these independents becoming a force in how we use our GPS units things can only get better from our view as consumers.

6 Which GPS should I Buy?

"Which GPS should I buy?"
The easiest question is always the most difficult to answer, because there is either no clear cut answer, or the short-cut answer of 'buy what I use'. Like with trying to advise which car to buy, a lot depends upon what you want to use the machine for. Recommending cars is easy; you need a tough 4X4 for off-road exploring (Land Rover Discovery), an MCC Smart can't be beaten for city motoring, while for long distance driving on tarmac you'd probably choose a VW Passat; easy isn't it, you have three cars. In GPS we  actually have four; two hand-helds for walking and two vehicle based units for road surveys.

Rather than recommend a range of models, or individual units, remember that to get the best use out of a GPS unit it is going to have to interface with other equipment and information. Virtually all consumer GPS equipment is USA designed, and manufactured in the Far East, meaning that the principal user in the designers eyes is American and the European market can get overlooked in specifying a particular design. Assuming that your main use for a GPS is for navigating in UK and European countries, and that you own a PC or Mac computer, here are the sort of questions you should ask before purchasing a GPS unit;

Which Map Datums does the GPS support?

In your "Baptism by Fire" you are taking information from an OS map and inputting it into your GPS for future use. If your GPS doesn't support the Datum of the maps you want to use then your main source of information cannot be used for GPS navigation without some complicated maths.

GPS units have a common default Datum of WGS84, the main American Datum.
For your UK use you will want OrdSrvy GB Datum available in your GPS.
In Europe you will need to use the Datums of the local maps. For DWG research areas we need the following Datums; SE Base for Madeira, Pico las Nieves for Canary Islands, European 1950 and European 1979 for mainland Spain and the Balearic Islands. We would never buy any GPS that did not support all the Datums that we anticipate using.

Computer Connection?

In "GPS - Advanced Use" we move onto linking your GPS to computer software, giving you much more navigational power. To do this you will need to connect your GPS to your PC. Modern PCs are dropping the slower communication ports in favour of USB. Check which communication ports are on your PC, and preferably not constantly in use for other equipment. With their 70s/80s technology most GPS units are still using a serial port for data transfer. If your PC does not have a serial port all is not lost as you can use a USB/Serial adapter but it mean you have another bit of kit to buy and look after.

Software Compatibility?

GPS manufacturers also produce GPS software programmes and Maps on CD, which are only compatible with their own equipment and software. If you wish to use the GPS software produced by independents then you will need your GPS to be compatible with that software. Over time this is seldom a problem as the programme designers update their software for new equipment specifications, though if you buy a new model of GPS when it is launched it might be some time before the software update becomes available.

What Accessories, and at What Price?

Accessories are available for all makes of GPS units, and generally they seem very expensive compared to the cost of the GPS itself. If you want to progress to 'advanced use' you will need a lead to connect your GPS to your PC, generally £15 - £30. You might want an external aerial, useful if using your hand-held unit in a car, and that's £35 - £55. A mount to clip your GPS to the handlebars of your mountain bike.

Think of the main uses for your GPS and then put together a total price package for the unit and the accessories.

It pays to shop around as you could find that Yacht Chandlers and Internet GPS Specialists offer better prices and have a wide range of GPS units and accessories in stock

Battery Life?

Hikers, and others, away from base for a number of days may have battery consumption as one of their priorities in selecting a GPS unit. If weight is a priority look at the units which use 2AA batteries as compared to 4AAs. Also remember that more functions, barometric altimeter and electronic compass, will consume more power. Batteries, as my own experience illustrates, vary considerably in their power capacity and have a lower capacity at lower temperatures.

GPS Memory Capacity?

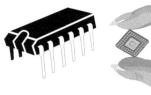

When you first start using a GPS memory capacity is always a worry as you wonder "Is the Track Log memory full yet?". I remember us spending a lot of time looking up the Track Log information during walks to see what percentage of the memory had been used. Never have we got anywhere near the limit of the track memory, 1024 track points, in a day's walking. Standard GPS internal memories are 500 Waypoints and 1024 Track Points.

  If you expect to exceed these memory capacities before being able to download the Track and Waypoint information to your PC then you have three choices;

- buy a laptop PC, or PDA, and take it with you, our own solution for walking research.

- buy a Datalogger, a memory device specially developed to be used with GPS to overcome the memory limitations.

- buy one of the GPS units with larger memory which are starting to appear on the market, such as Lowrance iFinder.

Will I Look Good With This?

Basically all GPS units do a good job of positional accuracy so your final choice might be based on what other people will think of your GPS.
Bright and Glitzy could give a modern image, or might be considered a bit toy like.
Matt Black is rugged with a military air, or could look old fashioned.
Garmin and Magellan are popular units so buying an Eagle or a Lowrance would mark you out as an individual.
 Carrying an expensive Trimble unit shows you're not afraid to pay top dollar for your equipment, or that you are a professional.

DWG Wish List for a Hand-Held GPS

12 Channel parallel receiver system. Large screen. Map Screen. Waterproof. Long battery (2AAs) life. All European datums. 16 separate Track Log memories. Optional external antennae. Large Memory. Fast USB data transfer. Upload maps from independent sources. Compatible with other hardware and software.

Well it *is* a '**Wish**' List!

7. GPS - Advanced Use

So far we've come a long way in understanding our GPS and in knowing how to use it in a practical situation. You could stay at this 'very competent' stage of GPS and quite happily enjoy the benefits of your GPS usage; calculating Grid References to produce Waypoint Lists for Waypoint Navigation, manually inputting the Waypoint Lists available in modern walking guide books such as Discovery Walking Guides '34 Walks' series.

All of this is very exciting, but you could get so much more from your GPS. Used on its own, and in conjunction with GPS Enabled maps (such as OS and DWG), you can achieve an advanced level of land navigation but you will always be limited to;
- Manually inputting Waypoints.
- Waypoint Navigation as compared to Track Log Navigation.

GPS, Computer Compatibility and Synergy.

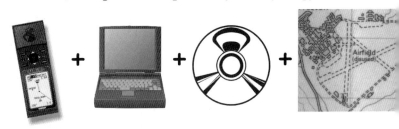

GPS + PC + Program + Maps = Navigational Power

'**Advanced Use**' of your GPS involves combining the power of modern computing, PC or Mac, with the navigational accuracy of your GPS through the use of GPS software. If you think your GPS is a pretty nifty bit of kit now, just see what you think when you go on to '**Advanced Use**'.

If you are thinking "and what's that going to cost me?" just think back to our exercise in GPS Navigation. Calculating Grid References and manually inputting them into your GPS is a time consuming exercise, and not really very exciting.

Now imagine you had that map on the screen of your computer 🖥, and as you move the cursor across the map it automatically calculates the Grid Reference; wouldn't that be wonderful - well you haven't heard the half of it yet.

Click your mouse 🖱 and you create a Waypoint, the programme calculating the co-ordinates for you. In seconds you can create all the Waypoints you need for a planned route. No more manually inputting to your

GPS, the software will download all the Waypoints you have plotted into your GPS in a fraction of a second.

Go into the Track function and each time you click the mouse  it makes a Track point. Simply click along your planned route to create a Track Log in the software. Again the software downloads this Track Log into your GPS in the twinkling of an eye. Now you can use Track Navigation with pre-planned routes, something which is impossible without software.

When you get back from your outdoor adventuring you can copy the Waypoints and Track Log stored in your GPS memory into the software and see exactly where you have been.

All of this is remarkable, almost unbelievable, until you have seen it happening, but best of all you can save all this information as computer files. Manual use of GPS means you are limited to one Track Log, and once you clear it the record is lost; same for your Waypoints.

GPS Software - Proprietary Programs

GPS manufacturers soon recognised the market for PC/Mac based software which could enhance the performance of their hardware. Unfortunately GPS manufacturers are notorious for the incompatibility of their products with other GPS manufacturers, those funny plugs on download leads are a good example, and this incompatibility has been extended to their software and maps. If you buy one manufacturer's hardware and software then you are likely to find yourself limited to their maps as well. It also means that if you change the make of your GPS the new unit is unlikely to communicate with the software.

Compatibility is a key factor in achieving the maximum performance from your GPS system. My own view is that Proprietary Programs limit compatibility and restrict your choice of mapping that you can use. My preference is for the Share-Ware Programs which operate with a wide range of GPS hardware and a wide choice of map sources.

If you still feel committed towards your GPS manufacturer's software ask what mapping is available, and at what scale and detail compared to OS maps, and ask the cost. You could find yourself paying more for the Map CDs than you have paid for your whole system so far, and still find yourself without enough detail to plot an accurate walking route.

GPS Software - Share-Ware Programs

A few enterprising individuals with an interest in the outdoors and GPS navigation also have considerable computer programming experience. These 'GPS Innovators' have applied their considerable skills to producing GPS software. The main Share-Ware GPS software programs;

Oziexplorer, GPSU, G7toWin and Fugawi, but other innovators are also producing GPS software.

Oziexplorer, GPSU, G7toWin and Fugawi have the common abilities of being compatible with a wide range of GPS units, accept map images in a range of formats, and allow Track Point and Waypoint editing to a reasonable level of detail. Oziexplorer, G7toWin and Fugawi also have CE versions which can operate with PDAs giving you a combination of moving map display combined with your GPS information; now that really is impressive.

Which of these you would choose to purchase is a very individual choice. I have worked with Oziexplorer and GPSU and my preference is for Ozi but there are plenty of people who prefer GPSU. G7toWin and Fugawi I have only read about in reviews. Whichever one you choose you will find plenty of GPS computing power for your money.

One over-riding reason to buy one of these share-ware programs is that in addition to the power they give to your GPS you will be to take full advantage of DWG's new 'Personal Navigator Files'.

"Memory Map" and "Anquet"

Two new products which have appeared shortly before writing 'GPS The Easy Way' are "Memory Map" and "Anquet" which appear to occupy the middle ground between the GPS manufacturers' software and the Share-Ware software.
All I know of these products is what I have seen in their adverts and the comments made in **uk.rec.walking** internet newsgroup. They seem more flexible than GPS manufacturer's software in that they support a range of GPS hardware, but you are limited to using maps purchased from "Memory Map" or "Anquet". Map designs are sourced from OS and Harvey and are available on CD 'from only £35' to £59.95 , and you will need a number of these to cover UK. Both systems are designed for UK use, unlike Share-Ware which can use any maps for anywhere.

Map Sources for Share-Ware Programs

Share-Ware GPS programmes can accept maps as images in a number of image formats. If you can acquire the map images then you can use them in your software for plotting planned routes and all the other functions available to you.

Main sources of map images are;
- scans of published maps eg Ordnance Survey.
- purchase of digital images on CD, again Ordnance Survey.
- download images from the internet, see 'Useful Internet Sites'.

When acquiring, and using, map images with your share-ware software you will need to calibrate the map image. For this you will need to know the map

Datum and the grid used on the map; for maps without a datum and/or a grid see '**Uncalibrated Maps**'.

After calibrating the map image you can start using the share-ware software for all its GPS functions.

It is tempting to keep one huge map image on your computer, covering everywhere you might want to go with your GPS but please try and resist this temptation. Big image sizes can slow down the programme when you want to scroll the map image to show an area currently off the screen. This 'slow scrolling reaction time' is very important if you use the software as a moving map display, for instance using a lap top computer and a GPS for a moving map display in a car; rather like a giant version of car 'sat nav' systems but without the annoying voice.

For a '**fast scrolling reaction time**' you should;

- if the software specifies a preferred image format, then convert your map image into that format using a 'Paint' program on your computer.

- keep your map image to the region you expect to use, eg Lake District will be a smaller image than UK at the same map scale.
It is better to have a number of compact images rather than one huge image.

- the smaller the computer memory taken up by the map image the faster it will scroll in the software.
Colour maps are super but they take up a lot of memory, convert the colour image into greyscale (Paint program again) and you will find it takes up considerably less memory, convert greyscale to Black & White and it takes up even less memory. This is a case of 'Appearance or Style' versus 'Efficiency'.

Uncalibrated Maps

Ordnance Survey, Harvey, Discovery Walking Guides and all national mapping agencies produce maps with Datum information and a grid either in UTM or Lat/Long co-ordinates. These are easy to scan and calibrate for your share-ware software, but there are lots of maps you might want to use that have no Datum information, or they might have a grid but no geographic co-ordinates.

To calibrate a map we need a minimum of three known geographic co-ordinates which are identifiable on the map image. In practice it better to have four co-ordinates and for these to be spread as far apart as possible on the map. The 'squarer' the co-ordinates the more accurate your calibration is likely to be, and conversely the more 'linear' the co-ordinates the less accurate your calibration is likely to be.

How DWG tackle Uncalibrated Maps;

- scan the map to create a map image. We normally scan at 300dpi in B&W, but if this loses detail try 300dpi greyscale, if there is still a problem with detail go to 300dpi RGB colour.
It may be necessary for you to change the settings in your scanning software to obtain good scanned images.

- if the map is bigger than one A4 scan then keep scanning until we have scans of the entire map area.

These images are then brought together in an image editing programme and aligned, then the finished map image is 'exported' as a TIFF image (for DWG software but use the image format required by your own software).

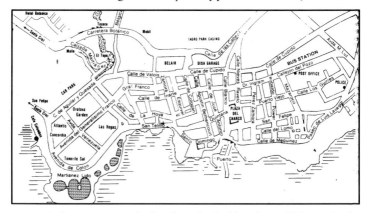

- we go to the map area and select four physical locations which are clearly identified on the map. At each location we power up the GPS, check that we have good satellite signals with at least two of the satellites in the outer ring on the Satellite screen, set the GPS Datum to WGS84, and 'mark' and 'enter' to record a Waypoint.

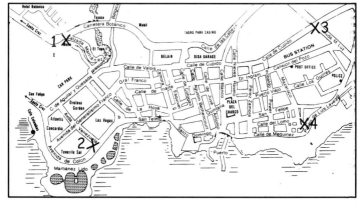

- after recording the four Waypoints it is back to the computer, or in our case onto the lap top, to bring the map image into the software for calibration. Remember the Waypoints are the values for a WGS84 Datum so set your Map Datum to WGS84 and assume a UTM projection.

- in your software mark each Waypoint position as a 'calibration point' and input the Waypoint location.

- with all four Waypoints as 'calibration points' ask the software to calibrate the map.

- now add a grid to the map. It doesn't matter if this is a UTM grid or a Lat/Long grid but have the grid size small enough so that you have a number North-South and East-West grid lines on the map image.

- What does the grid look like? The grid lines should cross at right angles. If they do then you have an accurate calibration and can use the map image with your GPS.

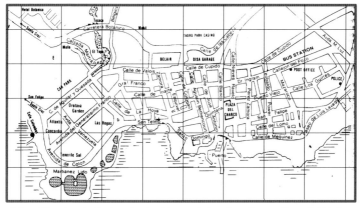

This calibration looks 'perfect' with North-South and East-West Grid Lines crossing at right angles, and with the Grid Lines aligned vertically and horizontally; but see later!

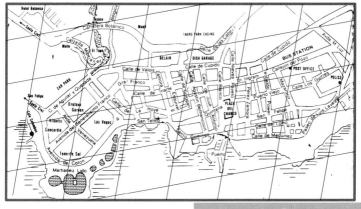

If your grid lines are noticeably not right angles then check the following items, one of which must be incorrect;

- Check that the Waypoint positions in WGS84 datum have been entered correctly as 'calibration points' in your software.

- Check that you have correctly identified the position on the map image as being where the Waypoint was recorded.

Note that if your grid lines do cross at right angles but the lines are angled then it means that the top of your computer screen is not the equivalent of North. You could still use your GPS software though angled grid lines can be disorientating.

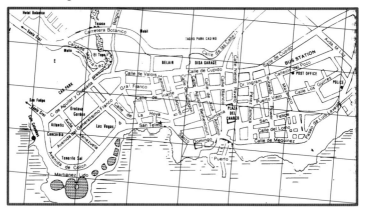

Best to estimate how many degrees rotation you need to bring the gridlines vertical and horizontal, then take the image back to your Paint program and rotate it by your estimate and resave the rotated image as the same name.

Now bring the rotated image into your GPS software and go through the calibration process again.

An easier way of achieving North-South orientation is to lay the map down in the region it relates to, rotate the map to agree with features you can see, then lay your compass on the map and mark the North-South line; there, you can't accuse me of being anti-compass!

Now let's have another look at the 'perfect' calibrated map again. This is a sketch map of Puerto de la Cruz in Tenerife. These are frequently drawn with the sea (Atlantic Ocean) at the bottom of the drawing, but it should look like:-

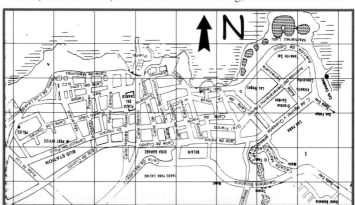

Summary of GPS Advanced Use

Specialist GPS software can greatly enhance the performance of your GPS through;

    - Rapid plotting of Waypoints and uploading those Waypoints to your GPS for use in Waypoint navigation.

    - Downloading of the Track Log and Waypoints from your GPS onto a map image to see where you have been; and the ability to save that information as computer files.

    - Creating a Track Log and uploading to your GPS for use in Track navigation, this feature is only possible using GPS software.

- GPS manufacturers software is normally only compatible with their own GPS units and maps.

- In UK "Memory Map" and "Anquet" systems may meet your needs for navigation in UK, but you may consider the maps expensive.

- Independently developed Share-Ware GPS programs offer the greatest level of compatibility between GPS units and map sources, and they are very sophisticated GPS software for the price.

8. GPS - Advanced Use
'Spencer Raceway' Practical Exercise

So now you have got your Share-Ware GPS software, and you are dying to see if it does all that I have been promising you. Actually it does a lot more but you'll soon find out how impressive it is.

For a Practical Exercise I will take you through the 'Spencer Raceway' image on the cover.

'Spencer Raceway' is an infamous piece of land on the Earl Spencer estate, lying between the Kings Heath housing estate on the northern edge of Northampton and Harlestone Firs a woodland with public access. 'Spencer Raceway' and 'Car Wreck Field' are famous for having the highest concentration of stolen and burnt out cars in the region, possibly in the country, and has featured on Anglia News.

Perhaps not the most attractive walking route I could have chosen, but an accurate map of this 'social phenomenon' might be useful.

A. Obtain Map Image

Knowing the area I wanted to cover I scan the OS 1.25,000 scale map of the area. If you haven't got a scanner then you could locate suitable maps on the internet.

When scanning always try to get as good an image as you can at the minimum memory. It is all too easy to lay a big OS map across the scanner, drop the lid and press the button; but the map can move or twist from its North-South orientation. To stop this movement I use 'Magic' tape to hold two sides of the map to the edge of the scanner screen. This might seem like fussy detail but after thousands of map scans I know it reduces my errors.

Check the scanner settings. I use 300dpi which gives good detail and allows reasonable expansion of the image on-screen in the GPS software.

For screen images scanning with a CMYK colour setting simply gives a big image with no advantage over RGB colour, so use RGB if you want a colour image. I like a greyscale image as the image size is smaller than RGB colour and the GPS information shows up better against the greyscale map detail. If you want the smallest image memory size scan in B&W, but you might have to experiment with your scanners 'halftone' settings to get a good level of detail.

Save the image file you have created as the file type that your software prefers eg jpeg, tiff etc.

If your scanned image is for a much bigger area than you intend to explore you can crop the image to a more manageable size in a

'Paint' programme. An A4 scan of a 1:25,000 scale map is equivalent to a land area of 7.3 kilometres by 5.25 kilometres; on a 1:50,000 scale map the A4 scan is equivalent to 14.6km by 10.5km, over 150 square kilometres of land area.

B. Calibrate Map Image in GPS Software

In my GPS Software (Oziexplorer) I go into the 'File' menu and select 'Import and Calibrate Map Image'. The program asks me where the image is, so I select my 'Spencer Raceway' image and this appears on the main screen with the 'set up' menu on the right.

In the 'set up' menu I select Map Datum 'Ord Srvy Grt Brtn' and Map Projection '(BNG) British National Grid'. Now my software knows what type of map we are calibrating.

Inputting Calibration Points

Now I select 'Point1' on the 'calibration' right hand section of the screen.

Then I move the cursor onto the map and select the intersection of the OS Grid Lines nearest to the top left corner of the map, and click to mark the intersection.

In the right hand 'calibration' screen 'BNG Coordinates' I input Zone 'SP' (found in the 'How to give a Grid Reference' section of the map legend), and

input the grid reference of the intersection as 'Easting 47300' and 'Northing 26400', and check that the 'N' is selected. Using the OS Grid References in the 'BNG Coordinates' is far easier than using the 'Degrees & Minutes' option.

Repeat this process for the top right corner and lower right corner of the map. With three accurately selected points I then click the 'Save' option.

Oziexplorer now calibrates the map and asks where I want to save the 'map' file. Best to save this 'map' file in the same folder that you saved the map image to.

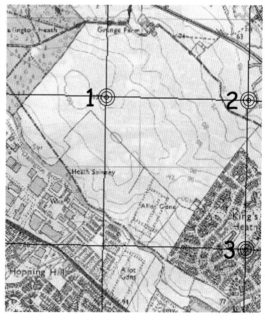

Note: the 'map' file only contains the calibration of the map image. When you load this 'map' file into the software it will call up the 'map image file' to which it relates. If you move the location of the 'map' file, or the 'map image file', then you will have to 'search' for these files when you next want to load them into the software.

Check Your Map Calibration

In the software select 'Map' in the top toolbar, and select 'Grid'. In the Grid options select 'Other' and a grid size of '1km' or '500m'.
Your Grid appears on the map and you have an option of colours for the grid lines.

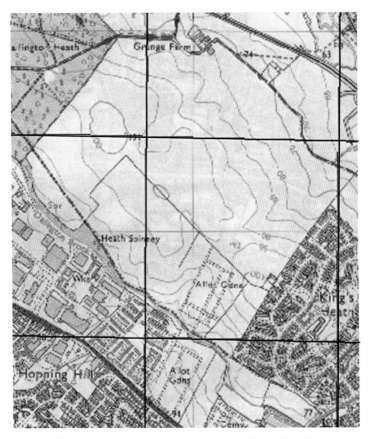

If your calibration has been correct then the 1km grid lines should lie over the OS grid lines of your map image.

If your lines agree with OS terrific, but if they don't then you need to correct your calibration.
'File' menu select 'Check Calibration of Map', back up comes the calibration screen.
Go through each calibration point carefully checking that you have input the correct grid references. A common source of error; I know!
Check you are operating in the northern hemisphere.
Check you are on 'Ord Srvy Grt Britn' datum and '(BNG) British National Grid' map projection.

Isn't It Wonderful!

The calibration screen disappears when you 'save' leaving a full screen view of your map image.

You can expand, or contract, the screen image using the '%Zoom' menu. With a 300dpi image you can expand the image to much larger than full size; meaning you can plot Tracks and Waypoints VERY accurately.
Good isn't it?

As you move the cursor over the map you will see a continuous read-out of the cursor's position in Lat/Long and UTM coordinates above the screen. You can find the coordinates of anywhere on the map in seconds.

Click 'Wpt' button on the tool bar and each time you left click the mouse it will make a Waypoint on the map.

Select a number of locations to Waypoint on the map.

Do you remember how long it took to calculate grid references from an OS map in our first practical exercise? Now you have selected all those waypoints in the time it took you to calculate one manually!

Waypoint List

Map Name : Northampton.tif
Map File : A:\NorthamptonUTM.map

Datum : Ord Srvy Grt Britn

Waypoint File : A:\SpencerRaceway.wpt

17/01/03 11:20:49

Num	Name	Zone	Easting	Northing	Alt(ft)	Description
1	001	30U	641441	5790925		16-SEP-02 08:22
2	002	30U	641407	5790976		16-SEP-02 08:23
3	003	30U	641320	5791171		16-SEP-02 08:26
4	004	30U	641305	5791209		16-SEP-02 08:27
5	005	30U	641405	5791387		16-SEP-02 08:29
6	006	30U	641436	5791356		16-SEP-02 08:30
7	007	30U	641533	5791279		16-SEP-02 08:32
8	008	30U	641550	5791261		16-SEP-02 08:32
9	009	30U	641482	5791181		16-SEP-02 08:34
10	010	30U	641606	5791281		16-SEP-02 08:37
11	011	30U	641581	5791280		16-SEP-02 08:37
12	012	30U	641591	5791301		16-SEP-02 08:38
13	013	30U	641596	5791302		16-SEP-02 08:38
14	014	30U	641600	5791299		16-SEP-02 08:38
15	015	30U	641609	5791302		16-SEP-02 08:39
16	016	30U	641638	5791332		16-SEP-02 08:39
17	017	30U	641678	5791370		16-SEP-02 08:40
18	018	30U	641805	5791533		16-SEP-02 08:42
19	019	30U	641967	5791726		16-SEP-02 08:45
20	020	30U	641482	5791380		16-SEP-02 08:54
21	021	30U	641470	5791385		16-SEP-02 08:55
22	022	30U	641303	5791545		16-SEP-02 08:58
23	023	30U	641296	5791547		16-SEP-02 08:59
24	024	30U	641280	5791557		16-SEP-02 08:59
25	025	30U	641273	5791557		16-SEP-02 09:00
26	026	30U	641274	5791562		16-SEP-02 09:00
27	027	30U	641260	5791558		16-SEP-02 09:01
28	028	30U	641256	5791558		16-SEP-02 09:01
29	029	30U	641197	5791641		16-SEP-02 09:02
30	030	30U	641093	5791721		16-SEP-02 09:04
31	031	30U	641091	5791743		16-SEP-02 09:04
32	032	30U	640987	5791849		16-SEP-02 09:06
33	033	30U	640948	5791891		16-SEP-02 09:07
34	034	30U	640882	5791917		16-SEP-02 09:08
35	035	30U	640863	5791894		16-SEP-02 09:10
36	036	30U	640847	5791855		16-SEP-02 09:11
37	037	30U	640750	5791796		16-SEP-02 09:12
38	038	30U	640733	5791769		16-SEP-02 09:13
39	039	30U	640707	5791729		16-SEP-02 09:14
40	040	30U	640678	5791680		16-SEP-02 09:15
41	041	30U	640677	5791673		16-SEP-02 09:15
42	042	30U	640656	5791666		16-SEP-02 09:16
43	043	30U	640657	5791661		16-SEP-02 09:16
44	044	30U	640649	5791668		16-SEP-02 09:16
45	045	30U	640638	5791652		16-SEP-02 09:17
46	046	30U	640620	5791658		16-SEP-02 09:20
47	047	30U	640640	5791638		16-SEP-02 09:21
48	048	30U	640642	5791635		16-SEP-02 09:21
49	049	30U	640623	5791636		16-SEP-02 09:22
50	050	30U	640599	5791634		16-SEP-02 09:22
51	051	30U	640600	5791619		16-SEP-02 09:23
52	052	30U	640577	5791581		16-SEP-02 09:24

Would you like a list of those Waypoints?
Click 'File' menu, select 'Print', select 'Waypoint List' and then choose whether you want your Waypoints printed with their **Lat/Long** or **UTM** coordinates, and **Print**; there a complete **Waypoint List** in seconds.

Already you should be convinced of the benefits of GPS software, if not you are very difficult to please.

Back to 'Spencer Raceway'

My intention was to plot the positions of all the burnt out cars as **Waypoints** and note their **'make & model'** manually; there's still a place for the biro and notepad even with this technology. At the same time I would record my **Track** which I could later edit as a **'guided tour'** of the phenomenon.

Starting on Mill Lane I powered up my GPS, waiting until I had full Satellite Acquisition.

PAGE **PAGE** **PAGE** **PAGE** to **Main Menu**, down to **WAYPOINT LIST** **ENTER** and then delete all Waypoints stored in my GPS.

PAGE **PAGE** **PAGE** page to **Map Screen** arrow arrow to **OPT** **ENTER**; check **Track Recording** is **WRAP** and then clear the Track Log.

Now I start off up the street on the western edge of Kings Heath Estate, Waypoint **MARK** **ENTER** where the path enters 'Car Wreck Field'. Wrecks are easy to see as I navigate along the official and unofficial paths criss-crossing the fallow fields, **Waypointing** each burnt out wreck and noting its 'make and model'.

'**Spencer Raceway**' is a dirt track carved out of the fields by the stolen car drivers. The drivers objective appears to be to 'tear around the track' as fast as possible and then ram the log-jam of burnt out wrecks in the centre, before torching 'their' own car.
120 minutes from starting out I am back at the field entrance and switching off my GPS **⏻**.

Downloading GPS to Software

Back at my PC I boot up the GPS software and load the Spencer Raceway map.
Plug my GPS onto the computer lead, which is left connected to the serial port, and press **⏻**.

PAGE **PAGE** **PAGE** **PAGE** **PAGE** to **MAIN MENU**,

down to **INTERFACE** **ENTER**,

down to **SEND** **ENTER**

down to **SEND TRK** **ENTER**.

On the software I select **Garmin** (that's how mine is configured) and select **Get Track**.
In a few seconds the Track where I walked appears on the map.

Next **Get Waypoints** and **SEND WPTS**, and up comes the sites of all those car wrecks; yes, there are a lot of them!

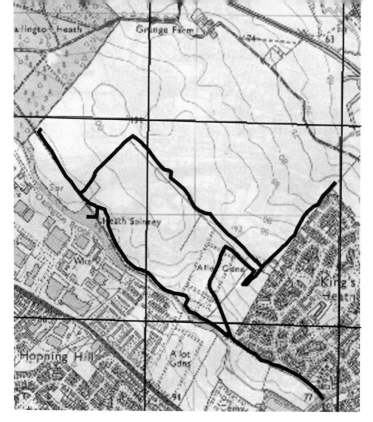

Track of my Walking Route for Spencer Raceway and Car Wreck Field.

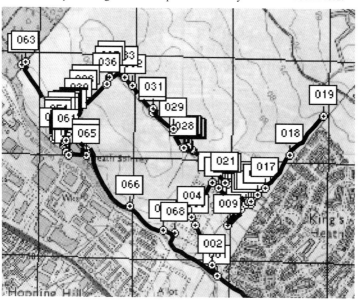

That's a lot of Waypoints and lots of car wrecks.

Miraculous.

Every time I download info from my GPS to the software I still think it is a miracle. The first time you download from your GPS you will probably be hooked on **'GPS - Advanced Use'**.

Spencer Raceway & Car Wreck Field

Surveyed: 16 September 2002.
Waypoints: 68.
Waypoint 001 taken at 08:22, Waypoint 068 taken at 10:18.
Total of 72 burnt-out car wrecks including 36 Fords, 20 Vauxhalls, 8 Rovers and 2 BMWs.
All 72 car wrecks were 'manual' transmission, no 'automatics'.
If there is a lesson to be learnt from 'Spencer Raceway & Car Wreck Field' it is probably that if you want to hang onto your car in NN5 then get one with automatic transmission!

9. GPS - Advanced Use
Plotting Track and Waypoints.
"Dallington Park & The Wheatsheaf"

A fellow 'aeromodeller' is visiting on Wednesday and knowing that we will end up in the pub for lunch I decide to plot a **Track** and **Waypoints** that will guide us around the local park and finish up in the pub. Brian has a Garmin 12 which he uses for retrieving free flight model aircraft (see Unusual Uses for GPS), but he has not seen any GPS software or '**GPS-Advanced Use**'.

This should be an ideal situation to show just what a GPS can do, and if we are successful we can celebrate in The Wheatsheaf.

Here is how I did it and whether we reached the pub.

A. Obtain Map Image and Cailbration

As we are close to the 'Spencer Raceway' I had intended using the same A4 scan of the OS Explorer 223 map that we saw in the last chapter and my map image is already calibrated. However as my original map scan was at 96dpi RGB colour, and for plotting Track and Waypoints I will need to expand the image in my software to get sufficient detail for accurate plotting I am re-scanning the area at 300dpi greyscale.

Note that the map sections shown as part of this exercise are just a part of the full map image; generally the larger the map the more accurate the calibration. Also the dark grid lines are the Lat/Long lines I have drawn on the map as I like to calibrate in degrees and minutes.

If you are unsure about scanning and calibrating a map image re-read 8 A & B.

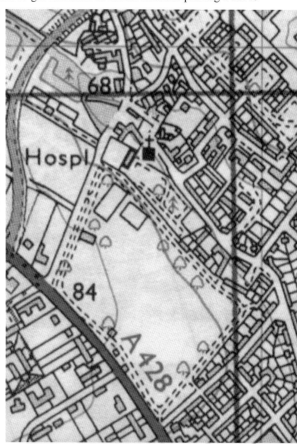

B. Plotting Waypoints and Track

To give us a bit of a stroll before reaching the pub I plot the Waypoints to give us an almost circular route. With the map at 300% zoom I can accurately plot the key navigation points of street and path junctions down to an accuracy of which side of the road I plan us to walk along.

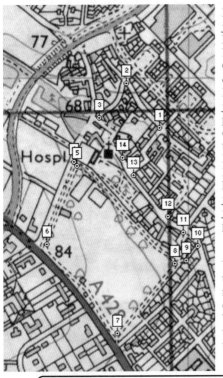

My planned route is; Wp1 junction of Tennyson Close and Brook Lane, Wp2 junction of Brook Lane and The Bartons Close, Wp3 Dallington village crossroads, Wp4 edge of Dallington Park, Wp5 path junction in park, Wp6 corner of park, Wp7 corner of park, Wp8 corner of park, Wp9 start of alley to Dallington Road, Wp10 onto Dallington Road, Wp11 Merthyr Road junction (and cross road here), Wp12 Cardigan Close junction, Wp13 Brook Lane junction, Wp14 The Wheatsheaf pub.

Yes, I know that we could get to the pub by a quicker route but remember the object of this exercise is to show Brian GPS Track Navigation as well as taking some refreshments after the exercise.

Waypoint List

Map Name   : Northampton.tif
Map File   : A:\NorthamptonUTM

Datum   : Ord Srvy Grt Britn

Waypoint File : C:\GPS\DallingtonPark.wpt

21/01/03 17:51:44

Num	Name	Zone	Easting	Northing	Alt(ft)	Description
1	1	30U	642183	5790419		junc Tennyson Close
2	2	30U	642085	5790539		junc The Bartons
3	3	30U	642012	5790447		village X roads
4	4	30U	641939	5790339		edge of park
5	5	30U	641953	5790325		path junction
6	6	30U	641867	5790107		corner of park
7	7	30U	642068	5789870		corner of park
8	8	30U	642224	5790055		corner of park
9	9	30U	642245	5790073		start of narrow alley
10	10	30U	642281	5790101		Dallington Road
11	11	30U	642254	5790144		junc Merthyr Road
12	12	30U	642198	5790192		junc Cardigan Close
13	13	30U	642105	5790295		junc Brook Lane
14	14	30U	642070	5790349		The Wheatsheaf

Once the Waypoints are plotted, and I have saved them as a computer file, I remove them from the map image before plotting the Track. Again I have got the map at 300% zoom so that I can plot the Track along the pavements I want us to follow. Moving the cursor along the planned route I click each time I want a Track point.

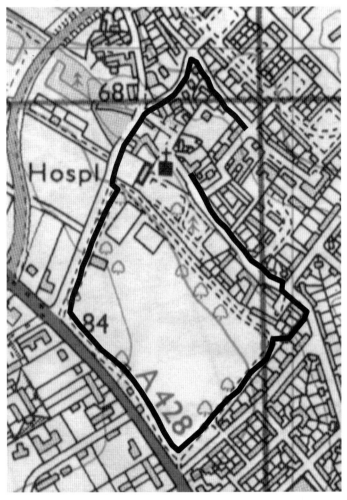

You could have a Track with hundreds, or thousands, of Track points; or only a few Track points with straight lines between them.

How much detail you put into the Track is really a balance between accuracy and time taken to prepare the Track. With GPS software you can easily input 30 Track points a minute, enabling you to build up a complex Track quickly.

For my Dallington Park exercise plotting of all the Waypoints and Track points took less than 5 minutes, compare that with the time to calculate 14 Waypoints manually for 'Waypoint' navigation and you will see why I love GPS software.

C. Getting to The Wheatsheaf via Dallington Park

Brian arrives to deliver the Russian model aircraft kit I had ordered and after coffee and chat we get ready for some **GPS Track Navigation** to get us to the pub.

I boot up my PC, call up the GPS software, and load the calibrated **Dallington Park map image** along with the **Track** and **Waypoints** files I have plotted for this exercise. On Brian's GPS  we clear the **Track Log** and **Waypoint List** so that there is a blank memory. While on the **Track Log Screen** I turn off the **Track Recording** so that the **Track** I am about to load will not get over written while we are walking. Now we are ready to load the **Track** and **Waypoints** I have prepared.

Plug **PC lead** into the **GPS**.

`PAGE` `PAGE` `PAGE` `PAGE` to **MAIN MENU**, down to **SETUP MENU** and `ENTER`, down to **INTERFACE** `ENTER`, down to **HOST** `ENTER`, down to **RQST WPT?** `ENTER`. **RECEIVING WPT** appears.

In the software I select '**Send Waypoints to GPS**'. Almost before you can blink the GPS is beeping to say that the transfer has been completed.

Back on **INTERFACE** screen, `ENTER` and then down to **RQST TRK?** `ENTER`. In the software select '**Send Track to GPS**'. A couple of seconds and the GPS is beeping again to say that the transfer has been completed.

Now we are almost ready to set off for the pub. As Brian has his GPS loaded with the Track and Waypoints I had prepared in the GPS software, and I have another GPS, I will use my GPS to record where we actually went and then I can compare the planned Track with the actual Track recorded on my GPS. So before we set off we check that we are in Mode Normal, Brian's Track Log recording is off and my Track Log and Waypoint List are cleared. All this just to go round to the pub!

There are two important things to remember about GPS Track Navigation.

First you must remember that the Track in your GPS is not like a 'Blind Landing' system and you will need your '**eyes and intelligence**' to make sure you do not walk into danger, such as crossing the road. When plotting the Track I have tried to put us on the pavements at the side of the street, but this requires 1 metre accuracy or better. So when the track would have us in the road it is only sensible to stay on the pavement. **GPS Track Navigation** is a **general navigation system** rather than a precise, exactly accurate system. The level of accuracy achieved depends upon GPS accuracy combined with how accurately the Track has been plotted, and this depends upon the accuracy of the map image and its calibration.

Second, choose better weather than we have got. Standing in the rain waiting for satellite acquisition it is very tempting to short cut straight to the pub.

It Feels Like Forever!

We are stood on the corner of Brook Lane at the junction with Tennyson Close (**Wp1**), with steady rain testing our outdoor gear, waiting for satellite acquisition; it seems to be taking forever.

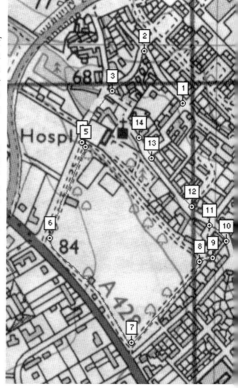

Apart from a couple of large trees (see Trunk Blocking earlier) there is only a dormer bungalow close to us, so where are the satellites. Both GPS' are getting three satellites, but it is a real struggle to get the forth and the rain is getting quite unpleasant.

My only consolation from this poor satellite acquisition is that we can't be anywhere near a cruise missile target, but we have a more worrying phenomena; the map screen on Brian's GPS is jumping about showing us somewhere near Waypoint 7!

Fearing that my map calibration is less than perfect we head back to the warmth of the PC screen. Boot up the GPS software, recheck the map image calibration; all is all right?

So its back out on the corner, in the rain, waiting for satellite acquisition.
All ready the 'fifteen minute' walk to the pub is ten minutes in and we haven't gone anywhere!
Tired of hanging around in the persistent rain we set set off with three good satellite signals (see **'Impatience' Cause of Inaccuracy** earlier) and a couple of blank bars hoping it will all work out. The **Map Screen** on Brian's GPS settles down and comes round to showing us going along the **Track**.

Following the **Track** left at **Waypoint 2** we come down across the village crossroads (**Waypoint 3**) and up to the edge of the park (**Waypoint 4**).
Apart from the start my plotted **Track** has been pretty successful but it is a concern at how quite small houses and big trees can reduce the satellite signals. At times we have had to use our 'eyes' to stay on the footpath when my Track would have had us in the road.
In the park it is more straight forward as we get better satellite reception, up to seven satellites, and the large trees are only having a minor effect.

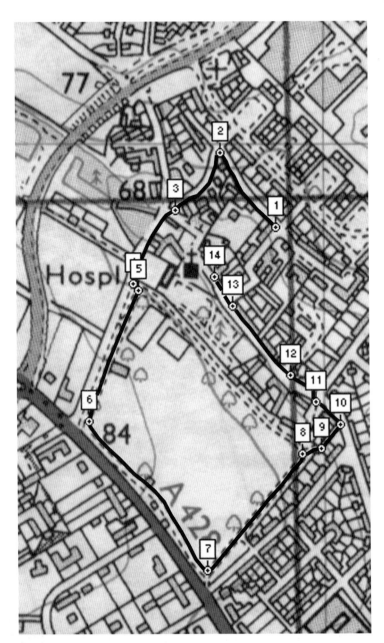

Waypoints 5, 6, 7 and 8 are easily navigated with Waypoint 9, and my Track, only slightly out for the entrance to the narrow alley. Down onto Dallington Road (Waypoint 10) to follow the track left past Waypoint 11, cross the road to pass 12 and 13 and finally, wet and none too comfortable, we are at Waypoint 14 entrance to The Wheatsheaf!

Review of 'Tracklog Navigation' Exercise

Our wet coats are dripping on the rack by the door as I get the drinks in. I feel morally bound to provide the refreshments as we have taken nearly thirty minutes, and quite a soaking, to get to The Wheatsheaf; which is only two minutes from Waypoint 1 by the most direct route!

Warm, dry and with a fresh pint, Brian is pretty impressed at our **Tracklog Navigation** apart from the problems at the start he reckons it is a very useful guide to navigating a pre-planned route; note, not 'perfect' but '**very useful**'. In the comfort of The Wheatsheaf we have plenty of time to review the concepts and practice of '**Tracklog Navigation**' when using a route plotted in GPS software.

Accuracy

Any Track and Waypoints plotted in GPS software can only be as accurate as the information they are based on. Inaccuracy can occur in scanning the map, the accuracy of the map itself, calibrating the map image, and placement of the Track and Waypoints on the map image. You would do well to get within 5 metres accuracy in plotting Track and Waypoints on a map image. Add in any inaccuracy due to poor satellite reception, or in our case '**impatience**', and we can see that GPS is not a 'Blind Landing' system.

Impatience

We should have known better, but in cold, soaking rain and thinking of the warm pub caused us to make the most basic error; '**impatience**' and moving off before we had full satellite acquisition.

Once we were on the move, with reasonable satellite signals, following the Track was straightforward. We must try to remember to put our GPS down with a clear view of the sky when it is switched on, and give it time to acquire four or more satellites **BEFORE** moving off, whatever the weather!

Eyes & Intelligence

GPS is certainly not a 'Blind Landing' system and following the plotted Track exactly would have had us walking in the road instead of on the pavement, or on the grass rather than the paths in the park, a few times. It would also have had us blindly crossing roads at Waypoints 3, 11, 12 and 13.

GPS might be good enough to deliver a cruise missile to its target, but it doesn't have to worry about traffic, roadworks, other people, tripping up pavements etc.

Satellite Reception

Apart from our foolishness at moving off before having four satellites, we followed the track without trouble, however even in Dallington village we had worries about satellite reception. While we didn't go down below four satellites, once we had acquired them (on the move), according to the bars on the Satellite Screen we were close to losing satellites at a number of points. Carrying the GPS at waist height it doesn't take a very big wall to block out satellites. Walking alongside houses noticeably reduced reception on the Satellite Screen.

Overall View of GPS Tracklog Navigation

Tracklog Navigation, with **Waypoints** for key navigation points, is an impressive aid to navigation. You can quickly see if you have gone 'off-Track'. Most inaccuracies come from the accuracy of the map, map scanning, map image calibration and plotting of the **Track** and **Waypoints**. These sources of inaccuracy are eliminated if the **Track** and **Waypoints** come from an actual GPS record of the route; as they do with DWG's **Personal Navigator Files (PNFs)**.

Walking a new route without a walk description can be unnerving for many people. Few are likely to completely rely upon GPS navigation, either Waypoint or Tracklog, preferring instead to use GPS as complementary to a written description. Similarly few walkers would set off, even with GPS, without familiarising themselves with the proposed route through a walk description and a map. GPS is likely to be used to complement current walking guide books and maps, to give a more accurate and reliable (given good satellite reception) means of route finding.

10. Personal Navigator Files (PNF)

Discovery Walking Guides is making a huge stride forward in walking navigation by producing **Personal Navigator Files** to complement its **34 Walks** series of walking guide books.

All DWG walking research is recorded as **Track Log** and **Waypoint** files. Already DWG publish Tour & Trail Maps and Drive Touring Maps which include Datum information and a geographic grid in Lat/Long or UTM format making these maps GPS compatible. DWG's recent walking guide titles all include GPS Waypoints, and the relevant Datum to input them into your GPS, for all routes with good GPS coverage.

Personal Navigator Files are a 'World First' in providing full Waypoints for all the walking routes (with good GPS coverage) in a 34 Walks guidebook. These Waypoints are in a format that is compatible with Share-Ware GPS software allowing you to upload them to your GPS via your GPS software.

For each walking route in a 34 Walks title the PNF includes a Track Log file, Share-Ware compatible, enabling you to upload the exact walking route to your GPS.

Using the Track Log file and Waypoints file for a 34 Walks walking route means you can use the Map screen on your GPS to navigate the walking route exactly as we researched it; well we do edit out our errors, see '**Compiling PNFs**'.

In addition to **Track Log** files and **Waypoint** files we include a '**Read Me**' with each PNF which explains the contents of the PNF and how to use the information.

Discovery Walking Guides and GPS Navigation

At DWG we were early converts to GPS, quickly recognising the value of pin-point accuracy for our walking guides. In the regions we research for walking guides the local mapping is very 'out of date' by up to 20 years or more and some local maps can seem more fiction than fact. We developed very detailed walk descriptions to help overcome the poor mapping, but were still forced to licence our base maps from the authorities and then add an overlay of corrections.

These base maps were not from just anybody, they were the official national mapping, equivalent to Ordnance Survey in UK; how lucky you are to have such good maps. Each time we licensed a section of a map for a walking guide the licence fee went up.

Faced with increasing licence fees for ever more 'out of date' mapping we called a halt and looked at producing our own maps. We spent a lean year juggling GPS equipment and software before we produced our first **Tour & Trail Map** at 1:40,000

scale. Since then we have improved research, survey and design criteria so that today our Tour & Trail Maps, Drive Touring Maps and Walkers' Maps are widely acclaimed as the 'most accurate' and 'clearest to use' maps available; and a long way ahead of any competing map. Without GPS we couldn't have done it. It was tough and stressful learning a new technology, new equipment and new computer systems but now we are seeing the benefits.

Nowadays we mix with a very varied bunch of people; walkers of all descriptions when we are out researching, and the MDs of some very big, and well respected, publishers of maps and travel guides. Even the MD of Ordnance Survey, will probably remember me as being that difficult bloke who asked 'Why don't Ordnance Survey ever put the selling price on their maps?' at a Barcelona mapping conference; OS still do not price their maps.

In such exhalted company it can be embarrassing for us when our map designs get complimented by MDs whose own company's mapping systems cost tens, or even hundreds, of thousands of pounds. By tackling the 'coal face' of accurate mapping personally, rather than hiring consultants, means that we have a massive lead over any walking guide publisher now looking to use GPS to improve the accuracy of their publications; and we intend to keep that technological lead.

Compiling Personal Navigator Files

All DWG's walking research is recorded on hand-held GPS units and downloaded into our survey software on completion of each walking route. We then closely examine the Track Log and Waypoint files for each walking route to compile our written description and map of the walk. At this stage the Track Log and Waypoint files contain all the information from the research including where we have gone wrong on a route and features of interest for our mapping which are not relevant to a walking route description.

Some Track Log files are unsuitable for publishing as a PNF due to poor, or inaccurate, GPS coverage; examples of this are the Barranco de Masca in western Tenerife where only 'vertical' satellites give poor positional accuracy compared to the narrow walking path, the upper reaches of Barranco del Infierno in southern Tenerife where there is no satellite reception, our town walks for Mao and Ciutadella on Menorca where 'building shadowing' gives intermittent satellite reception which would require you to stop and reaquire satellites if relying on GPS navigation alone
.

From our Track Log files we edit out the wrong turnings and extraneous information so that the new Track Log shows the walking route as it is described in our **34 Walks** guide book.

For the Waypoint file we edit out the extra information Waypoints so that the file agrees with all the waypoints in the **34 Walks** written description.

The result of this detailed editing are **PNF Track Log** and **Waypoint** files that you can use for **GPS Track Navigation** to follow the DWG walking route.

PNF Accuracy

DWG's walking guides cover a range of walking routes from easy up to expert status in a range of exciting destinations. All of DWG's walking destinations are linked by the poor quality of the 'official' mapping available for these regions. Official maps are usually 'out of date' by up to 20 years, and frequently inaccurate in showing routes which do not exist. Often our walking route is following a clear trail not shown on any map until DWG publish a new map of the region.

Inaccurate, out of date, maps mean that you cannot use your GPS software to plot a planned route from the 'official' maps. Well you could plot a planned route but it is unlikely to be of much use. In these circumstances there is only one way to accurately record a walking route and that is to walk it with your GPS. The result of this accurate walking research are DWG's **Personal Navigator Files**.

As a publisher of walking guides we often suspect that the writers of other guides have not actually seen the route they describe. Requiring our authors to use GPS, and our software, means we know exactly where our authors have been, they have walked all the routes we publish and we have the Track Log to prove it.

PNFs are designed to compliment a **34 Walks** guide book and its **Tour & Trail Map** or **Walkers' Maps**, as appropriate. Our PNF files are the most accurate way of describing a walking route and you could use them in your GPS as your only navigation aid, but we do not recommend this approach. Walking is much more than just an accurate method of getting from one place to another, it is about the whole 'walking experience'.

DWG Maps will give you an overview of the region you will be walking in. **34 Walks** guide books tell it as it really is for our authors; you won't find descriptions such as 'relaxed stroll', 'relentless ascent', 'round the hairpin bend we face one big mother of a gradient' in a PNF.

PNF Compatibility

PNFs are designed to be used via Share-Ware GPS software and are supplied in a file format compatible with these programmes. You simply down load the Track Log and Waypoint files to your GPS software and then upload those files to your GPS.

PNFs are not compatible with "Memory Map" or "Anquet".

PNFs are 'Datum Independent' thanks to the Americanisation of GPS units. All consumer GPS units store the position information for Track Log and

Waypoints in WGS84 datum co-ordinates. When you change the GPS Datum your receiver converts the WGS84 co-ordinates into the equivalent co-ordinates for the Datum you have selected and displays these as your position. Thanks to the commonality of WGS84 default datum it does mean that PNFs will work with any Datum.

With a PNF loaded in your GPS and following Track navigation on the Map screen you will be following the correct walking route irrespective of whatever Datum you have selected.

If you want your position co-ordinates to be compatible with the **Waypoints Lists** in **34 Walks** guide books, and with **DWG Maps**, you will need to set your Datum to the one quoted in the book or on the map.

Limitations for PNF use

PNFs are a huge stride forward for navigating walking routes wherever there is good GPS coverage.
In practice the limitations you will face are;

- incompatibility of GPS software if you are using GPS manufacturer software

.
- your GPS only having one Track Log memory, limiting you to only one walking route Track Log being in your GPS receiver. You can load each walking route's PNF Waypoint file as a Route, and call them up as you need them. To load a new PNF Track Log for a new route you will need to use your GPS software, which is why you find DWG writers, and PNF users, using lap-top computers in unusual locations

.
- PNFs are copyright protected and are licensed for 'personal' use by the purchaser.
Publishing copyright lasts from the date of publication to 70 years after the author's death; so if you illegally copy or publish the PNF information we, or our executors, will be suing you for breach of copyright damages.

11. Unusual Uses for GPS

Retrieving Free-Flight Model Aircraft

"You take this model aircraft, which took ages to build, and then you launch it into the air, and it flys away. No radio control or anything?" I know it sounds crazy but this is my hobby when not grinding out walking routes. The object is to put your model aircraft into a thermal, a rising column or bubble of hotter air, and then when you want the model aircraft to come down a timer causes the tail to pop-up; causing the model to descend in a controlled stall, the process being called a 'de-thermaliser'.

That's how it should work. All too often the timer doesn't work, or something hooks up; we've been doing this 'de-thermalising' for over forty years and we still can't get it to be reliable! Or the rising thermal is going upwards faster than the model aircraft is trying to go downwards when de-thermalised; result model aircraft continues ascending until the thermal cools and disappears.

The result is a model aircraft some distance away, it could be up to twenty miles or even more. Now Free-Flight model aircraft flyers are more genned up than it sounds so far in that most of us use radio tracking devices, tiny transmitter on the aircraft and hand-held receiver, but the range is limited so we normally need to be within a kilometre of the model for the receiver to pick up the signals.

GPS aided model recovery works by taking the compass line of the model in flight when last seen; my sighting binoculars are used for model aircraft, not 'map & compass' navigation. I input a waypoint into my GPS on this compass heading at a projected distance of twenty kilometres and activate the GOTO function. Then it is into the car to drive after the model. On the Map screen I can see whenever the road I am on crosses the model's flight-line; stop get out and look with the binoculars and switch on the radio receiver. If there is no visual sighting or radio signal then it is back in the car to drive further down the model's flight line, and this is repeated until we find the model.

Balloon and Glider Recovery

How I wish my wayward model aircraft could phone me with their precise position, then I could just go directly to where they are and pick them up. This is just what happens for the pilots of hot-air balloons and gliders landing in the countryside. Phone your retrieval crew with your GPS position. They input this position into their GPS and activate the GOTO function. Then they follow the same search method as for my model aircraft except they have a precise location rather than a search line.

Competition Glider Flying

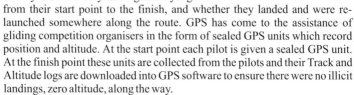

In cross-country gliding competitions it can
be very difficult to say how a glider flyer got
from their start point to the finish, and whether they landed and were re-
launched somewhere along the route. GPS has come to the assistance of
gliding competition organisers in the form of sealed GPS units which record
position and altitude. At the start point each pilot is given a sealed GPS unit.
At the finish point these units are collected from the pilots and their Track and
Altitude logs are downloaded into GPS software to ensure there were no illicit
landings, zero altitude, along the way.

Geocaching

Being able to specify precise locations, in geographic co-
ordinates, then means that others with GPS systems can
guide thamselves to the pre-determined location. This
rather bizarre activity, and I say that as one who flies free-
flight model aircraft, has become known as 'Geocaching'. Normally the
cache consists of a guest book for you to 'sign in' that you have found the
geocach. It appears to have originated in California and you can find websites
dedictaed to providing geocach locations, so if you've got nothing better to do
at the weekend you could go 'geocaching'.

Treasure Trove - Ocean

GPS has been a real boon to those intrepid 'treasure
hunters' of the oceans. Prior to GPS these modern
bounty hunters had to mark their Spanish galleon,
once they had found it, with a flotation buoy. To
return to the wreck they would use their old system of
'map & compass' navigation to get to the general
area and then look for the buoy marking the wreck.

Of course the problem was that anyone else could
also find the buoy, and the wreck, and by the time you
returned it might be that your dubloons had already
disappeared into some modern pirate's hold.

With GPS you simply waypoint the position above
the wreck. When you want to return to the wreck you
simply input the waypoint into your GPS and use
GOTO to return to the exact spot on the featureless ocean.

Treasure Trove - Land

Treasure hunters on land seldom use GPS to mark the position of a potential hoard, relying upon the land's physical features to return to the search area. But we have all seen those comedies where after the bank job, and hiding the loot, the gang are caught and jailed. After their sentence they return to where they hid the loot only to find the entire area has been redeveloped and all the original landmarks have disappeared.

How much easier for the modern 'blah, blah, blah, Rio de Janeiro' blaggers to simply waypoint where the loot is buried. When they want to dig up the ill-gotten gains simply activate the waypoint in the **GOTO** function and you'll soon be ready for that flight to Brazil.

Researching Walking Guide Books and Maps

It is quite amazing the navigational power at your fingertips with a GPS unit combined with GPS software. At DWG we think it is the greatest thing since the compass, but this view is not common in the 'outdoor adventure' publishing business.

It's not just the MDs who think that GPS is not relevant to walking or navigational books; it is the authors as well. We know a number of 'walking guide book' authors, there aren't that many of us covering Spain, and none of them use GPS; you did read that correctly "none of them use GPS"!

Even when they have seen our GPS units and software in operation they are unconvinced of its value. Actually its an 'age' problem. All the authors we know were brought up on 'Map & Compass' navigation and have reached that 'Meldrew' time in life where they don't want to have to learn a new skill from the bottom up. DWG, by comparison, have developed a tutoring system for our new authors which quickly gets them up to 'GPS Expert' status. It seems as if our technological lead over other publishers is likely to increase, rather than decrease.

From the comments we have received from publishers and walking authors along the lines of;
"GPS is nothing to do with navigation." Yes, this really was said to us.
"I've only met one walker with a GPS and he didn't know how to use it." Well once that walker has worked his way through "GPS The Easy Way" there will be another GPS convert.

Unbelievable, simply unbelievable that walking authors think that the most accurate system of recording a walking route, GPS + software, doesn't apply to their work. It looks as if the 'World of Walking' is going to split into two species; the 'old dinosaurs' and the modern 'DWG and other GPS equiped' authors; so at the moment "Researching Walking Guide Books" is an 'Unusual GPS Use' or in those classic words 'I don't believe it!'.

Glossary

2D Mode	GPS receiver operating with only 3 satellites, inaccurate position.
3D Mode	GPS receiver operating with 4 or more satellites, accurate position (usually).
Acquisition	GPS acquiring, and locking onto, satellite signals.
Bearing	Compass direction to a destination.
Datum	Cartographic reference on which map coordinates are based.
DGPS	Differentially corrected GPS.
Easting	Distance East of the map origin in a UTM coordinate system.
ETA	Estimated Time of Arrival.
ETE	Estimated Time Enroute, time to destination at present speed.
GPS	Global Positioning System.
Grid	Parallel map lines for a coordinates position system on a map.
Initialization	Power up process for a GPS to find its position.
Latitude	North/South measurement of position in degrees from the equator.
Longitude	East/West measurement of position in degrees from the Greenwich meridian.
Magnetic North	Direction a compass needle points when not affected by magnetic interference.
MOB	Man Overboard function of a GPS.
Navigation	System of planning a travel route and correcting direction while enroute to reach a planned destination.
NAVSTAR	US Defense satellite system that provides the signals for GPS receivers.
Northing	Distance North of the map origin in a UTM coordinate system.
OS	Ordnance Survey.
PNF	Personal Navigator Files.
Route (in GPS)	A collection of Waypoints stored in a GPS for navigating a route.
SA	Selective Availability; the degradation of NAVSTAR satellite signals to reduce GPS accuracy to approx 50-100 metres.
Topographic Map	Map that presents both horizontal and vertical information eg height points, contour lines.
Track	GPS record of its route.
True North	Direction of a line of Longitude.
UTM	Universal Transverse Mercator. A standard rectangular grid system used between 80° South and 84° North. The earths surface in these limits is divided into 1,000 kilometre grid squares.
Waypoint	Position location saved in GPS memory.
WGS 84	World Geodetic System 1984. Main USA datum and default datum of GPS receivers.

Map Datums for European Land Navigation

If you wish to use your GPS with UK and European maps then it is advisable that your GPS supports the following map datums:

Datum	Country
CH-1903	Switzerland
European 1950	Austria, Belgium, Denmark, Finland, France, Germany, Gibraltar, Greece, Italy, Luxembourg, Netherlands, Norway, Portugal, Spain, Sweden, Switzerland.
European 1979	Austria, Finland, Netherlands, Norway, Spain, Sweden, Switzerland.
Finland Hayfrd	Finland.
Ireland 1965	Ireland/Eire.
Obsrvtorio '66	Azores.
Ordnance Survey GB	United Kingdom.
Pico de las Nieves	Canary Islands.
Potsdam	Germany.
Qornoq	Greenland.
Rome 1940	Sardinia.
RT 90	Sweden.
SE Base	Madeira.
SW Base	Azores.

GPS on the Web

The Internet is a tremendous resource for everyone seeking information, and if you do not have an Internet connection we recommend that you get one. If the Internet has a disadvantage it is that there is 'too much information' and it is all to easy to get confused by the sheer volume of conflicting views on any topic you can think of. Type 'GPS' into a search on the Google search engine and you get 5,630,000 web addresses to look through!

Joe Mehaffy

Given this overwhelming volume of information we could give a very long list of interesting websites, but it would go out-of-date as soon as we had finished typing the list. Better to concentrate on a few sources which discuss GPS issues and one website which has become a legend in Internet GPS. Joe Mehaffy seems to have been into Internet GPS since the early days and soon built up a reputation for independent reviews of GPS hardware and software along with a general discussion of GPS issues and problems. His original site at http://www.joe.mehaffy.com has expanded over the years (a very long time in Internet terms) until it has become too large for its original site and has now been transferred to its own server at:-

http://gpsinformation.net
Bookmark this site as a major net resource of GPS information. If the site has one problem it is in being American based. Normally this isn't a problem except when it comes to discussing the maps available from GPS manufacturers. USA topographic maps are freely available giving GPS manufacturers a low-cost source for their own map products. By comparison European mapping from GPS manufacturers is very limited.

Internet News Groups

It's always good to seek the opinions of like minded people, and if you can't find any of those you can try an appropriate Internet News Group. A couple of News Groups deal specifically with GPS:-

sci.geo.satellite-nav
deals with all GPS issues with a world-wide coverage though mainly American input. Logging on to this news group you will be stunned at just how much there is to discuss about GPS hardware, software, compatibility, leads etc.

alt.satellite.gps
is another GPS newsgroup but is mostly a mirror image of sci.geo.satellite-nav but with less postings into the news group.

Walking & Cycling Newsgroups

If you are into walking in the UK then you should subscribe to:-
uk.rec.walking
where you will find a wide range of opinionated opinions along with a lot of helpful discussion. It is interesting to see how opinions on GPS have changed within this news group over recent years. At one time to mention GPS was to

attract a torrent of disapproval (and that's being diplomatic) but gradually opinion is changing. Now the uk.rec.walking news group is evenly balanced between those who insist that "Map & Compass" is real navigation (despite compasses only having an accuracy of +/- 2 degrees) and GPS users. GPS users on the news group can offer valuable practical advice on GPS hardware and software use for UK walking, some news group members are well into PDA based moving map GPS navigation systems; but don't forget that **uk.rec.walking** is primarily a 'walking' discussion group rather than a GPS resource.

alt.rec.hiking
is an American based news group mostly discussing US based hiking with little mention of GPS.

uk.rec.cycling
is a UK based cycling discussion group covering commuting, road racing, mountain biking from cotter pins to saddles. Surprisingly GPS does not seem to impinge on the thoughts of UK cyclists.

Internet web sites generally are no place for the unwary. Internet News Groups, especially, seem to attract a certain type of opinionated opinion which you would not get in a 'face to face' discussion, though this has been moderated in the groups mentioned above. Be aware of the Internet's limitations and you have access to the greatest body of information; some excellent, some good, some useless, some bad, ever assembled. GPS fits well with this new millenium technology.

www.streetmap.co.uk & **www.multimap.co.uk**

Both of these web sites provide an excellent mapping service covering the UK. You can search the UK by place names, post codes, grid references for a map of the area, which you can see in a range of scales up to 1:25,000; and these 1:25,000 map sections are OS maps.
In theory you could build up a 1:25,000 scale map of UK by capturing images from these web sites, though it would take you some time even on a broadband connection and even then you will have to bring all the seperate images together and calibrate the resulting giant map. For use with your GPS software you are probably best sticking with OS paper maps, but for finding out where somewhere is these sites are unbeatable.

Share-Ware

Oziexplorer, GPSU, Fugawi & **G7toWin** will all be selected from a search of the web. Also see the reports on Joe Mehaffy's excellent site **http://gpsinformation.net** where you will find many more Share-Ware reports. If you are looking for a simple Waypoint and Route management program, which is free, try **EasyGPS**. New software is being developed all the time making it impossible to say just what will be available when you read this.

DISCOVERY WALKING GUIDES

PERSONAL NAVIGATOR FILES

Getting lost is not a pleasant experience, while getting lost in a foreign destination can be distinctly unpleasant. DWG have an excellent reputation for accurately researched and described walking routes, but even we can go further with our revolutionary **Personal Navigator Files**.

All DWG's **34 Walks** series of books are researched using modern GPS equipment, giving us an accuracy of better than five metres. GPS gives us extremely accurate walking routes, and DWG knows exactly where our authors have walked. Now we are making this GPS Track and Waypoint information available for GPS users in a range of formats to suit popular GPS software such as Oziexplorer, GPSY, Fuginawa.

If you have a GPS, download lead and GPS software for your PC, then DWG's new **Personal Navigator Files** will mean that you can follow in the exact footsteps of our walking authors; now that really is 'vorsprung technik' for walkers.

Personal Navigator Files are available for:-

- **Alpujarras**
- **Tenerife**
- **Lanzarote**

- and will be available for all new **34 Walks** destinations. For more information, see DWG websites:-

www.walking.demon.co.uk
and
www.dwgwalking.co.uk

DISCOVERY WALKING GUIDES

TRAIL & TRAIL 1:40,000 SCALE MAPS

Tour & Trail Maps were developed to meet the needs for accurate and up-to-date maps for destinations covered by Discovery Walking Guides. At the core of each **T&T** map design is a comprehensive ground-level survey carried out by car and on foot. The survey results are then translated into DWG's design programme, to produce a digital vector graphic database involving the organisation of several million pieces of information across a large number of 'layers' drawn digitally within our computers. Once a DWG digital vector graphic database has been established, new developments such as new roads and tracks, can be quickly incorporated into the correct layer of the database. Rapid updating, combined with state of the art 'file to plate' pre-press operation, enables DWG to produce new editions of **Tour & Trail Maps** quickly and efficiently.

Tour & Trail Maps have a Latitude/Longitude grid and datum information making them GPS compatible. DWG walking routes are clearly highlighted on **T&T** maps, along with their GPS Waypoints wherever space allows.

From 2003, all new **Tour & Trail Maps** titles will be produced on a super-durable material which is waterproof and tear-proof, making **T&T** maps the toughest maps available, in addition to being the most accurate and up-to-date.

Tour & Trail Maps are available for:-

- **Alpujarras**
- **Madeira**
- **La Gomera**
- **Gran Canaria Mountains**
- **Mallorca North & Mountains**
- **Menorca**

DISCOVERY WALKING GUIDES

34 WALKS

- a series of Walking Guide Books

We receive praise for our regional walking guide titles in almost every post. Thanks to the many happy users of these guides, DWG has acquired an enviable reputation for interesting and accurately described, walking routes. Now the time is right for our new **34 Walks** series of walking guide books. These new books are wider ranging than our previous guides, covering whole islands or regions. All the routes have been newly researched and even our 'classic' routes have been re-walked and rewritten to ensure that they are up-to-date.

Each title in the **34 Walks** series is designed to provide a wide range of interesting routes for moderately fit walkers, plus some routes for experienced walkers. Thanks to the feedback we receive from walkers we have designed these books so that you have the best walking guide book for the destination. Features in **34 Walks** books include:-

- walking route summary
- fully detailed walk descriptions including frequent timings
- GPS Waypoints (grid references) for all key points on a route
- detailed map at 1:25,000 or 1:40,000 scale for every walking route
- full GPS Waypoint lists for all the walking routes

Add in useful background information, and you have the best value walking guides that you can buy.

34 Walks books form one part of DWG's complete walking package. For each title there is also a **Tour & Trail Map**, or **Walkers' Maps** to complement each book.

Available from good book shops or by mail order. For up to date information on Discovery Walking Guides publications write to DWG Ltd, 10 Tennyson Close, Northampton NN5 7HJ, England or visit:-
www.walking.demon.co.uk or
www.dwgwalking.co.uk

DRIVE! TOURING MAPS

Drive! Touring Maps are designed for today's drivers with the emphasis on accuracy and clarity. Using the digital vector graphic databases from our **Tour & Trail Maps**, plus specially commissioned surveys, **Drive! Touring Maps** are completely up to date on publication. Being up to date is important as Spain has recently changed its road numbering system, which makes driving very confusing if using an old map.

Special design criteria have been developed which result in exceptional clarity, while emphasising the motorist's needs for quick recognition of junctions, road numbers, petrol stations and refreshment stops with off-road parking.

Each **Drive! Touring Map** includes:-
- a comprehensive Place Name Index
- a Distance Chart for main destinations
- datum and grid information enabling the map to be used with modern GPS equipment

All this is backed up by:-
- large scale Street Plans which include Place Names Indexes for major resorts

Drive! Touring Maps include everything you need for exploring these exciting destinations by car.
Drive Touring Maps are available, or in development (D) for:-

- **Tenerife**
- **Lanzarote**
- **La Gomera** (D)
- **Gran Canaria** (D)
- **Fuerteventura** (D)
- **La Palma** (D)
- **Madeira**
- **Mallorca** (D)
- **Menorca**

INDESTRUCTIBLE MAPS

We've all suffered from maps that fall apart, split down the folds, and soak up water like a sponge. Sellotape, or better drafting tape, is pressed into service to repair the ailing paper map to try and make it last a bit longer. At DWG we believe in durability but even we admit that our paper maps have a limited life when subjected to the rigours of outdoors adventuring. So putting our money where our mouth is, we have formed **The Indestructible Map Company Ltd (TIMCo)**, which does exactly what it says in the name; it produces **Indestructible Maps** which are 'Guaranteed for Life'.

TIMCo combines DWG's expertise in researching and designing the best maps, with the latest materials technology and printing techniques, to produce the **Indestructible Map**. They tell us that the material is a 'high density polymer' core to which they fuse a printable layer of a China Clay type compound; well, they lost us somewhere around 'density' but we do know that what we have got is a map that in 'normal' use will last you a lifetime. It is waterproof, tear-proof, and just about proof to everything apart from fire and attack with sharp objects. You can fold it into a rain hat or beer glass - we've tried, so we know it works - and then still use it as the best map. It feels like silk but appears to have the strength of carbon fibre. You get all of these attributes in an **Indestructible Map** and all at a ridiculous price of £4.99.

Indestructible Maps are not easy to produce - otherwise all map publishers would be using these materials and techniques. Paper is easy. It has been around for hundreds of years and printing paper has been highly developed, plus paper is cheap. Specially coated high density polymer is expensive, eye-wateringly expensive. Printers don't like polymers; they have to run their machines more slowly (more expense), use special inks (very expensive) and put special dryers between each stage of the printing process.

On the first print run of **Tenerife Indestructible Map** our printers forgot some of the complex settings and 455 copies of **Tenerife Indestructible Map** fused themselves into a solid indestructible lump; unfortunately the printers dumped the mistake or we might have been short-listed for the Turner prize!

After all this, you have a lovely **Indestructible Map** as a flat sheet, but that is not the end of your problems. Folding an Indestructible material is a real problem as it always remembers that it once was a flat sheet; TIMCo have to keep the boxes of printed maps sealed until use otherwise we have a lot of flat maps which were once folded!

Enough of the moans and whinges about producing **Indestructible Maps** - just try one for yourself. We are convinced that TIMCo is the future of maps, and we will be using these materials and techniques for DWG's new **Tour & Trail Maps** and **Walkers' Maps**.

www.indestructiblemap.co.uk

New to accompany our **34 Walks** series of guide books is a series of **Walkers' Maps** at a 1:25,000 scale, 4cms = 1km, a scale that is so popular for UK walking.

The interesting walking regions for destinations such as Lanzarote and Tenerife form pockets around the island, and a whole island **Tour & Trail Map** would not be viable; Tenerife at 1:40,000 scale would make a 3 metres by 2 metres map and Lanzarote would only be a bit smaller. Just try unfolding something that size while out on a walking route!

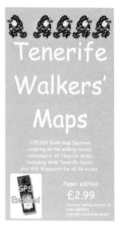

To solve the problem of providing top quality mapping at a pocketable size, we have developed **Walkers' Maps** which bring together the walking regions at 1:25,000 scale onto a single folded map at a size to fit your pocket. This gives you large scale maps for all the routes in a **34 Walks** guide book in one map product.

Tenerife Walkers' Maps will consist of 1:25,000 map sections covering routes in the South (4 map sections), West (one large map section), Las Cañadas/Teide (3 map sections) and the North (one large map section) plus an island locator map. The full **Tenerife Walkers' Map** and **Lanzarote Walkers' Map** are published in two editions; a low cost Paper edition and a Super-Durable waterproof and tearproof edition, using the same materials and techniques as for **Indestructible Maps**.

INDEX

INDEX